"*The Revolution* does not merely make the case for social justice, but offers practical action steps that Christians can put into practice."

—FREDERICA MATHEWES-GREEN,
Beliefnet.com Columnist

"This book is a spiritual kick in the pants. It challenges. It educates. It offers solutions and hope. Even better, it annihilates my own isolated, me-first faith. This is a book I'll be buying in bulk and giving away."

—JASON BOYETT, Author of *Pocket Guide to the Apocalypse* (RELEVANT Books)

"For those of us working for the abolition of torture, the inclusion of a chapter on this terrible crime against humanity is welcome, indeed. This issue and the other eleven discussed in the book make a solid reminder that if the world is to be made better, we must be the ones to do it. And to do it, we must act."

—SISTER DIANNA ORTIZ, OSU, Torture Abolition and Survivors Support Coalition International (TASSC)

"This powerful book is crammed with inspiration and practical information about how regular people taking small steps are creating surprisingly influential forces for positive change. *The Revolution* is a must-read for any person of faith who feels called to take an active role in helping tackle our global society's most deeply rooted problems."

—ROSE BENZ ERICSON, Author, Fair Trade Resource Network Co-founder

THE
REVOLUTION

A Field Manual for Changing Your World

EDITED BY Heather Zydek

[RELEVANTBOOKS]

Published by RELEVANT Books
A division of RELEVANT Media Group, Inc.

www.relevantbooks.com
www.relevantmediagroup.com

Design by Relevant Solutions
Cover design by Ben Pieratt and Jeremy Kennedy
Interior design by Jeremy Kennedy and Ben Pieratt

RELEVANT Books is a registered trademark of RELEVANT Media Group, Inc., and is
registered in the U.S. Patent and Trademark Office.

For information or bulk orders:
RELEVANT MEDIA GROUP, INC.
100 SOUTH LAKE DESTINY DR., STE 200
ORLANDO, FL 32810
407-660-1411

Library of Congress Control Number: 2005934262
International Standard Book Number: 0-9768175-2-7

06 07 08 09 10 8 7 6 5 4 3 2

Printed in the United States of America

CONTENTS

FOREWORD

BY JIM WALLIS

On the speaking stump, I often refer to myself as a nineteenth-century evangelical born in the wrong century. Evangelical Christians at that time combined revivalism with social reform to help lead the campaigns to abolish slavery and establish women's suffrage and child labor laws. That tradition continued into the twentieth century with the civil rights movement, which was, of course, grounded in the black churches. It is a very encouraging sign for the future that many Christians of the twenty-first century, especially younger generations, are rediscovering this tradition of faith and action for social justice.

I was surprised when my book tour for *God's Politics: Why the Right Gets It Wrong and the Left Doesn't Get It* resulted in book signings-turned-town meetings and book store events-turned-revivals. I realized something important was happening that was about more than a book. *God's Politics* was simply the right book at the right time; it revealed what was already there across the nation, just waiting to be expressed. Many people of faith felt their voices were not being heard in the national debate over religion and politics and now found something to point to.

The strong message of the book also pointed to the essential moral and spiritual character of many of the most pressing issues our society confronts—the massive nature of global and even domestic poverty, the crisis of the environment, the cost and consequences of war, the selective moralities of both the Left and Right in regard to the sanctity of life, and the breakdown of both family and community.

We now face a new moment of opportunity and must rise to the occasion, both spiritually and politically. Those responding to this opportunity come from across the religious spectrum. They are evangelical Christians who don't feel represented by the ideological religion, shrill rhetoric, and divisive behavior of the Religious Right—now being rejected by a new generation of young evangelicals. They are Catholics who believe that abortion is a moral issue and are committed to dramatically reducing it, but believe the rest of Catholic social teaching and a "consistent ethic of life" are also important. They are mainline Protestants who desire a deeper integration of a personal faith and social gospel. They are black Christians who bring a historic and holistic gospel, and Hispanic and Asian Christians who dream of a genuinely multicultural future.

These issues being raised are the matters at the heart of *The Revolution: A Field Manual for Changing Your World*. Poverty—both global and domestic—is the most unifying and galvanizing issue. Overcoming poverty is seen by many, especially young people, as the natural outcome of faith, even test of faith in our time. Protecting the environment—God's good creation—is a deeply rooted and growing commitment that is especially important to a new generation of young Christians. The critical need for a "moral response to terrorism" and an alternative to unilateral and preemptive wars such as the one in Iraq is becoming more and more apparent as the deaths increase and policy failures are revealed. There is growing unease with the partisan manipulation of issues surrounding the sanctity of life, where politicians from the Left and Right use the issue for their political advantage rather than seriously address the real threats. And the fraying bonds of our closest relationships in family and community, which might be attributed to the rise of selfishness and harsh individualism that continues to undermine the common good, raise deep moral issues.

The writers in *The Revolution*, many of whom are friends and colleagues of mine, address these issues in a powerful and hopeful way. They provide the information and analysis necessary to understand the issues, as well as the creative ideas on what to do about them. *The Revolution* is, most importantly, a book about action—what can be done about the biggest social problems we face. As the subtitle states, it's "a field manual for changing your world." And, significantly, the essays here are all rooted in a deep faith that informs each author's social and political commitments. This book illustrates the truth that social movements with the best chance of making a difference are most often rooted in spirituality.

The Revolution is a book I heartily recommend to all who want their faith to help make a better world.

JIM WALLIS is author of *God's Politics: Why the Right Gets It Wrong and the Left Doesn't Get It*, editor of *Sojourners*, and convener of Call to Renewal.

INTRODUCTION

BY HEATHER ZYDEK

As I write this, every cable news channel is on overdrive, fixated on one thing: the devastation caused by Hurricane Katrina after the Category 4 storm slammed into America's Deep South. Hours and hours of footage air throughout the day, mobilizing viewers to help those affected by devastating flooding. Meanwhile, pundits pontificate about our government's willingness (or perceived lack thereof) to help the mostly poor, black population stranded in a watery wasteland. Floods of money pour into major charities' coffers from generous citizens. First responders and socially conscious journalists flock to the scene. And compassionate folks everywhere lament the tragedy.

Every season has its Katrina-like disasters—some natural, some man-made. From hurricanes and terrorist strikes to the quieter, perpetual disasters like hunger, AIDS, and human trafficking, societal ills of all kinds are ever-present and great. But greater is the love that can overcome these ills. If God is love, and if we are made in His image and likeness, surely there is enough love in this world to wipe away every tear that falls from the eyes of those afflicted by pain, hunger, war, or some other misery.

But how do we collectively tap into that love? What are the ways, both broad and specific, that we can address human strife, human need? And what barriers often stand in the way of us doing so?

I am not a social worker, professional activist, or sociopolitical scholar. I've never run a major social-justice nonprofit. I'm just a nearly-thirty-year-old journalist with a specialty in community and social-justice reporting who happens to find myself asking the same questions over and over again about service, voluntarism, and charity. The questions vary from time to time, but all revolve around a common, two-pronged theme: what does it mean to serve the "least of these" as Christ asked us to do, and how exactly does one do this in a meaningful, real way?

In all the ruminating I've done, I've come to some basic conclusions about myself and, perhaps to a certain extent, my generation when it comes to charity:

WE'RE QUICK TO RESPOND, BUT ALSO QUICK TO FORGET.

Our generation is moved by intense, dramatic displays of horror and injustice—and we may be willing to open up a vein and start giving until we're drained of all our blood ... for a few days, anyway. Then the memory fades as quickly as our favorite cable news network jumps to another set of news alerts, and for us, life soon moves on to more exciting things.

WE'RE MEDIA-MOVED PEOPLE.

A movie vividly depicts genocide, and we're immediately online as soon as the credits roll, making a donation to GenocideOrganizationX.org. We see coverage of a terrorist attack unravel on cable TV, and we head to our blogs to post supportive banners. A poignant series on famine in a foreign country has us ready to board a plane with suitcases full of food. Individual crises that become media sensations compel us—but everyday, perennial tragedies like international hunger or poverty simmer quietly in our social subconscious.

WE WILL GIVE FREELY— AS LONG AS IT DOESN'T HURT.

We are heartened by outings to serve meals at homeless shelters—especially when we can enjoy a fine dinner at a posh restaurant afterward (if you think I'm making this up, I'm not— I've seen it happen). We love giving big, generous donations to charity while savoring the richness of the sweet tax write-off such donations bring, come April 15. In this country, we love to have our cake and eat it, too. Like the law-abiding rich young man in Matthew 19 who wanted to do "good," we struggle to give up our own comfort to heed the call of Christ; we're constantly looking for easy and/or indulgent ways to give. But as Mother Teresa said, "I hope you are not giving only your surplus. You must give what costs you, make a sacrifice, go without something you like, that your gift may have some value before God. Then you will be truly brothers and sisters to the poor who are deprived of even the things they need."[1]

WE DON'T HAVE TIME.

We're hyper-scheduled and overbooked, working sixty, seventy, even eighty hours a week to bring home the proverbial bacon. All this work leaves little time for band practice, book clubs, sporting events, church meetings, and classes. Oh, and, of course, "me" time. To quote from the VeggieTales' "Good Samaritan" cartoon, "We're busy, busy, dreadfully busy. You've no idea what we have to do. Busy, busy, shockingly busy. Much, much too busy for you."

WE'VE GOT BAGGAGE.

Our hearts and minds are burdened by internal conflict. We feel the guilt of living in varying degrees of comfort while our peers half a world away dress in rags and eat little more than dust. Self-analytical to a fault, we constantly wonder whether we are driven to serve out of guilt; a longing for warm fuzzies; a hero-complex to validate our otherwise spoiled lives; or—as it should be—by a genuine, selfless, long-suffering love. On top of this, it's hard to reconcile our comfortable lives here in America to the lives of those we serve—uneducated people born and raised in poverty, who refuse to depart from what we see as self-destructive, ill-informed lifestyles and don't want to be "saved"; people who will gladly take a handout but don't make any effort to positively change their lives for the long haul.

WE'RE CONFLICTED IDEALISTS WITH CYNICAL ALTER EGOS.

We center a lot of our beliefs about how Christians should treat others on the "social gospel" proclaimed by Christ in Matthew 25, yet we can't help but wonder what Christ meant when He said, "The poor you will always have with you, but you will not always have me" (Matt. 26:11, TNIV). And we can't quite reconcile that teaching with the goals of most international anti-poverty campaigns that would eradicate poverty—and actively plan to do so.

If I sound like I'm doing nothing but finger-pointing, be assured that I point the finger first and foremost at myself. I'm as guilty as any other GenXer of being deficient at offering real help to my brothers and sisters in need. And I certainly don't claim to have valid answers to any of these problems. I'm sure I could spend pages expounding upon various theories on how compassionate, bleeding-heart Christians like myself might be able to combat these challenges. However, I'd be a big phony if I pretended that any answers I might offer came from anything other than armchair theorizing.

This is precisely why I've asked the twelve writers of the essays in this book to contribute their unique thoughts on why social justice is important and how the particular problems they address might be tackled by the average citizen. These writers, along with the foreword and afterword writers, are all highly knowledgeable activists, theologians, and scholars who have dedicated their lives' work to serving the "least of these."

From serving the poor on the street to lobbying our goliath government to use its wealth to feed the world's poor, these activists have experience to share and stories to tell about some of the most pressing ills facing humanity today. They come from different Christian traditions (some Catholic, Eastern Orthodox, Evangelical) and tackle different issues in their daily work, but they share a unified vision: for every reader who delves into this text to heed the call to action out of a deep and real love for others.

I compiled this book so that it can motivate as well as inform— these authors don't just explain what the problems are; they offer practical ways to help those afflicted by the crises. The twelve essays all end with details on how to take action; the afterword further explains how to take a stand for the poor, sick, suffering, and needy; and the appendices will give additional direction on how to get involved in serving others.

This book isn't an exhaustive treatment of social justice; in fact, it would take volumes to include essays on every social ill present in the world today. *The Revolution* is meant to be a concise handbook that points people in the direction of action; where you go from here depends on how motivated you are to learn about the many different ills that plague our world.

My prayer is that each and every reader will find something illuminating in these pages about how and why to die to self, reach out, and lovingly and prayerfully care for all of God's precious creation, on every possible level.

This is the revolution that must take place—it is not a worldly revolution through which we strive to create some soulless communist machine. It is instead a personal revolution, a communal revolution; above all, it is what Mother Teresa once called a "revolution of love." Instead of relying on anger, bitterness, and even violence to spur action to bring about change, we—militants of this revolution of love—use heavenly, God-ordained weapons of charity, love, peace, and willful self-sacrifice to serve others using the richness of our talents, knowing that even though only God can eradicate all the world's ills in His time, while we're here on this earth, we can each fulfill His ultimate command to love our neighbors as ourselves.

In XC,

HEATHER ZYDEK
September 2005

TAKING ACTION, IN FOUR EASY (AND SOMETIMES NOT-SO-EASY) STEPS

While all societal ills have different remedies, action can be broken down and applied based on these four easy-to-remember steps:

DONATE

There is a mind-boggling array of organizations that need monetary donations to finance their work in service of those in need. One of the most basic ways to help in a time of need is to donate money and other resources to social justice organizations. See the resources section (Appendix C) in this book to find contact information for a variety of different charities and relief organizations to which you can make a one-time gift or become a regular contributor, or find a local charity you like and set aside a portion of your monthly income to give to that organization.

EDUCATE

First, educate yourself—learn everything you can about an issue that resonates with you. Then, teach others in your various social circles to take action. Finally, consider becoming a formal educator, speaking publicly about the issue and what can be done to help.

ACTIVATE

Get up off your comfy armchair and make a differ-ence. This is your chance to be the kind of servant that Christ's most ardent disciples have been throughout the history of the faith—sacrificing their own wants and needs to help others. There are many ways—from the simple donation of a few hours of your time each week to an all-out vow of poverty—to engage in the arduous but fruitful work of serving others. Again, Appendix C, along with your local yellow pages, should give you plenty of ideas on how to donate your time and energy in the service of others. Also remember to get active on the political level, as going to the source of a problem often means going to your local, state, and federal government officials and encouraging them to propose and pass legislation that will change laws in favor of those in need.

PRAY

Last but not least, pray. Pray proactively, pray reactively, pray for strength and wisdom in bringing aid to the direst of situations. Pray that God, in His abundant mercy, will help us to accept His good and perfect will, even when it doesn't seem too good and perfect to us. Pray in thanksgiving and rejoice when God extends His grace to His suffering children, enabling them to overcome adversities despite the odds. Pray before moving and pray after. Prayer is our most valuable weapon in our war against evil.

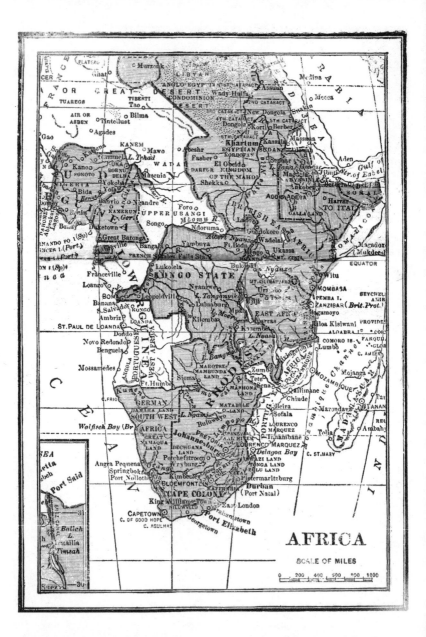

AFRICA

SCALE OF MILES

0   200   400   600   800   1000

CHAPTER ONE

CLEAN WATER

BY DAN HASELTINE

"A PESSIMIST, THEY SAY, SEES A GLASS OF
WATER AS BEING HALF EMPTY; AN OPTIMIST
SEES THE SAME GLASS AS HALF FULL. BUT A
GIVING PERSON SEES A GLASS OF WATER AND
STARTS LOOKING FOR SOMEONE WHO MIGHT
BE THIRSTY." —G. DONALD GALE

Two times a day. It was a four-hour journey, and most of the women and children made that walk twice a day. No time for anything else. Not even a moment's respite from the heat of the afternoon. Just walking and carrying. What they carried was a liquid in conflict with itself, a liquid sharing two diabolical identities—life mixed with death. It was both cure and poison.

Inside the bucket was a mixture of water, dirt, algae, cow and goat feces, bacteria, mosquito larvae and other insect eggs, parasites, and various waterborne diseases waiting for a host. This is what they walked miles and miles to carry back to their homes. It was a Trojan horse, except most of the women in the village knew that the enemy was hiding in the gift.

The choice, which was really no choice at all, was not to drink the water and die, or drink the water and live and, after a while, die. And every person in that village had to make this choice or, as was the case for many children, have the choice made for them.

I watched as the women and children of the village walked with ease, a callousness that must have built up over time. They had strong necks and hard heads. We still had nearly three miles left to travel.

DONATE
Help fund a water project in an African community.

We walked across dusty terrain, over hills, and through thickets of brush and rocky fields, winding our way across the ground, the shell, the barrier that held below its surface what everyone in that village needed: clean water.

Perhaps that was the most frustrating part of the experience. Water—clean, healthy water—was just out of reach. Below the ground we walked upon was a wealth of cool drinking water. Like children stretching themselves to reach a cookie jar that had been placed just barely out of reach, these Africans knew there was a cure to the stomach problems and the opportunistic diseases and the constant walking and carrying. It was simply a matter of digging deeper than hands could dig. It was a problem that, because of the firm grip of poverty, had lingered in the minds of everyone in the village as unfixable. It cost money to dig a well; it required leadership and organization; there had to be a working knowledge for maintenance procedures and the ability to develop strong plans for economic growth. It was too hot, and people were too sick and too poor and too hungry. Help mostly came in such unreliable and inconsistent forms that any sustainable plan for well construction seemed a distant impossibility and any dreams or real conversations about children free from parasites and dehydration were veiled by the dusk shades of diminished hope.

I rubbed the sweat from my forehead with the thin towel in my hand. What would it take to come alongside these people and help them reach the clean water they desperately needed? How many other villages and communities shared a common story? How can it be that a world as small as ours still holds places where people barely hang on to life and so often die for need of something as basic and as easily accessed as clean water?

THE DISCONNECT

As I attempt to share with you the simple and the complex building blocks of the water crisis in Africa and other developing lands, I am aware that our nation is vastly different, and to many of us it is incomprehensible to find that there are nearly three hundred million people in Africa who do not have access to safe drinking water. However, to riddle a conversation with grossly tragic statistics—even if they do provide a fuller picture of a crisis—would, I fear, simply cause you to care less. And at this place in the timeline of eternity, Americans do not need any more reasons not to care. Cultural barriers can be almost insurmountable to those of us in America who have never thought about dying from a lack of drinking water.

Even if our minds allow us to envision an African child digging a hole in the sand far enough to reach a pool of brown water, sticking his face down in it, and, in an act of survival, drinking, we struggle to move from the feelings of shock or compassion toward a movement of practical care and humble action. Water is just not something we worry about. And those who do worry about it are the kinds of people so far off our radar and so profoundly different than us that we can only come up with feeble pictures in our heads about them. In America, bottled water accounts for 66 percent of the nonalcoholic beverage market, far outselling coffee, soda, and sports drinks like Gatorade and Powerade. We do not wake up wondering if we will have enough water to drink—consumerism has made sure of this.

The growing multibillion-dollar bottled-water industry has flooded the supermarkets and convenience stores with more choices in clean water than ever before. We do not have to be satisfied with water from the tap. We do not have to deal with high levels of iron, lead, fluoride, or chlorine. Our bodies stay properly hydrated, so our complexions are smooth and blemish-free; our skin is softer and our muscles have the kind of elasticity necessary to perform in an active environment. Our hair is stronger and healthier; our digestive systems function with regularity; even our brains function more efficiently, giving us an increased threshold for concentration. But water is not just a healthy choice; it is a fashionable one. Water is branded in ways to accommodate any kind of lifestyle. It is as unique to us as the music we download or the coffee beverages we order.

But in parts of the world beyond the reach of the bottled-water industry, there are twenty thousand funerals a day for people who struggled to survive without access to any form of clean water or proper sanitation. The symptoms of this crisis are vast and heartbreaking.

In an orphanage outside of Kenya, a child squirms during a

reading time. She excuses herself and goes to the bathroom. She lifts up her dress, pulls her underwear down, and finds a worm. It is four inches in length. It was pushed out of her body by other worms, as this type of worm only leaves when there is overcrowding. The worm eggs are ingested in the water she and the rest of the children drink. The parasites grow inside of the digestive tract, causing malnutrition.

Nearly all of the children from the orphanage have these worms. This particular orphanage does not have a clean-water well, so the women running the orphanage and the children are forced to drink, cook, and clean with the egg-infested water that is available.

"How wonderful it is that nobody need wait a single moment before starting to improve the world."

—ANNE FRANK

Although, on the surface, the provision of water seems basic enough, it has its complexities, as do all issues of community development. Clean water is an issue compounded by poverty, geography, and lack of leadership and resources. But the greatest hindrance to finding viable solutions is the deficiency of personal relationships. There is a humble approach to community development, but it has taken years of failure to figure out.

In the 1980s a massive initiative centered on the construction of clean water wells, irrigation, and sanitation systems across the continent of Africa. Those water projects were the result of a grand-scale proclamation dubbing the 1980s "The International Drinking Water Supply and Sanitation Decade" (IDWSSD). Governments and non-government organizations turned their attention to the growing crisis of water unavailability and the lack of proper sanitation. The goal was to decrease the number of people without access to these basic needs by roughly 300,000 people a day. The programs and projects of the 1980s were able to nearly meet the established goals: they provided clean water and sanitation for almost 250,000 people per day.

But in less than six years, many of the sanitation projects and clean-water well systems that contributed to those figures fell into disrepair; many of the projects from the IDWSSD were too poorly managed to provide for the basic needs of upkeep; and people within the communities did not have the maintenance training necessary to keep the water systems functioning properly. By the late 1980s, many water pumps installed for irrigation were unused due to a lack of spare parts, water supplies were polluted by sewage, and the water crisis was again on the rise.

EDUCATE
Talk to people at your church, school, business and in your community about the issue of clean water and motivate them to take action.

History has shown us that unless our solutions to community-development problems allow Africans to take ownership of a project, there can be little hope for sustainable, effective growth in a community. Many clean-water projects fell into disrepair simply because the organizations that built them failed to acknowledge the true needs of the community. If we approach community development in a cultural environment foreign to our own without the appropriate humility, we will fall into the trap of making development decisions based on our own cultural history and environmental context, instead of that of the community we intend to benefit. If we do not pursue personal relationships that can foster local leadership, and if we do not insist on indigenous ownership and stewardship, then we will not have the proper groundwork to build a well or sanitation system that will provide lasting community growth.

There have been many success stories about communities that have taken responsibility for their own development. In the remote regions of Kenya, groups of women form water teams. It becomes their responsibility to begin the groundwork for constructing a well in their community. They are the women who take care of orphans and nurse the sick and those dying from AIDS. These women identify and develop leadership in their villages. They raise funds to bring in a team to test the soil and the ground to see where the well should go. They arrange for the drilling team to bring the equipment needed to dig. They establish maintenance teams and set in motion a plan to raise funds through the sale of water, once the well is operational, to others in the community. If they sell the water at a reasonable cost, they can raise the necessary funds to do repairs on the well or buy food for orphans or start up small capital ventures that can prepare the community to work on microfinance programs. The women in these communities understand that a well is not simply a handout, but rather a huge incentive for them to take initiative, find creative ways to break the cycle of poverty, and shed the victim mentality that hangs over their villages like a thick fog.

THE EFFECTS

The presence of clean water has life-saving effects. Within weeks, villagers notice the absence of stomach problems, and children do not have diarrhea or the pain and exhaustion of malnutrition—clean water flushes out worms and other parasites. Over a short time, hygiene practices can be implemented, and the overall health of a community increases. The food is healthier, and there is more of it, so their bodies are capable of building up stronger immune systems that can fight off all kinds of opportunistic diseases. Cleaner, healthier communities have a much greater chance to thrive, as there is greater potential for villagers to be more productive.

In time, the improved health and productivity of the people will give way to indigenous, creative community development, and this can foster better leadership and even better organization of health-care facilities and business.

"Let those who are thirsty come; and let all who wish take the free gift of the water of life."

—REVELATION 2:17, TNIV

The gift of time is an essential benefit to a community with a clean-water well. Once water is accessible, days normally spent walking and collecting water are used for education and vocational training. People have time to learn a trade or craft. It is truly amazing what water can do.

Just as a man on a white horse coming to town gives hope to a village of terrorized citizens, so water brings hope—and hope does not disappoint. Water is a building block of life and civilization; it is at the heart of industry and commerce. Those who do not have it die; those who do, live. And with life comes greater life.

Transforming a community from a hopeless land of funerals into a place of hope and life is hard work, and it's work that cannot happen without real people making choices that reflect a worldview informed by the life of Jesus Christ. The only sustainable forms of humanitarian service are born out of real relationships and the desire to listen and walk humbly with those in need.

It takes time to build relationships. It takes time to organize water teams, train people to maintain a well, and construct water systems. And unless we have a desire to serve people outside of our own communities, we will never have the time to do these projects right. At this point in the story of African peril, Americans continue to be distracted by cultural and color differences, religious complexities, wars to support or discourage, and abortion and homosexuality to rally for or against. Meanwhile, the window of time to know and love gets shorter, and we find that the vast ocean separating our continents has made it nearly impossible for us to remember that Africa even exists. Those of us who do not forget must find reasons to care, offering up reminders to others so that they can feel the humanity underneath the issue.

And why do we care? Because those who suffer are our brothers and sisters, our mothers and fathers, our children and grandchildren who lift their cries to the hungry African skies. I cannot simply ignore knowledge gained for the purpose of action and wisdom that demands response. When I begin to imagine what it would be like to hear my children cry and picture myself hopelessly watching as they become frail and weak and breathless, my heart won't let me go to the end of that place.

It was reported that in the unforgiving environment of concentration camps scattered throughout Nazi-occupied Europe, the sound of crying babies was piped over loudspeakers as part of the torture and unimaginable cruelty during World War II. Jewish prisoners would slowly go crazy, unable to sleep through the relentless noise while overcome by the effects of forced sleep deprivation.

The sound of a suffering child has no soothing characteristics. It carries with it the rhythm of unmet needs. It is urgent and irregular. It is a builder of tension upon tension, a fertilizer for helplessness that grow like kudzu in the nerves, tangling itself into the eardrums, fatally wounding the soul. Hearing the prolonged sound of a helpless child on the verge of death is like accepting the entrance of a silver bullet into a cavern of the heart. And the longer the sound remains, the deeper the bullet claws, until it is so far inside that it actually breaks its way into the fortress of our needless, wantless American souls. Waves of air originate in the miniature gut and lungs of a child, and the sound that these vibrations produce is powerfully vile and tragically offensive to our very being.

THE CONNECTION

Over the course of a weekend in September 2005, America was touched by what much of the rest of the world had long experienced. Many communities in Louisiana, Mississippi, and Alabama were destroyed by the vengeful hammer of a Category 4 hurricane named Katrina. It was a modern-day Vesuvius, trading the choking clouds of ash and slithering lava for the freeform amoebae of wind and water. Television screens flashed images of homes submerged and histories carelessly blown away. The shock of such unfathomable loss left expressionless faces as the appropriate filler between tragic stories, rising death tolls, and impending deficiencies of proper shelter, food, and clean water. When the levees crumbled and flood waters rose, the scattered masses who had not heeded the call to evacuate began to sense that this was not a fight they could simply wait out. Rather, they were being pushed into the ring of one of the most magnificent and historic mismatches—humanity, entrenched and half-poised, versus the giants of wind, rain, and natural fury. When the skies cleared, the sun gave light to a shredded coastline and a new Atlantis, a city underwater. The landscape had been altered, and the rich and the poor—now unified and indistinguishable in their merging story of survival—mourned the loss of familiar streets and family heirlooms. The shelters began to fill, and in the churches, stadiums, and other remaining buildings, people gathered and reunited, feared and mourned.

In the nights that followed, as people tried to sleep, it was not the sound of relief workers, ambulances, or the rattle of nerves that kept people awake—it was the sound of children. The effects of dehydration and hunger pains were starting to set in, and so the cries began. The news teams did their best to communicate to the world the sense of growing urgency and desperation that hung in the air as a new fear took root. It was an unexpected fear: the fear of our own children, children of the most resourceful nation in the world, dying because they did not have clean water to drink. In a land destroyed by a surplus of water, throats grew raw and thirst was unquenched. And rising out of the mud, sewage, and flooded streets came an unmanageable thirst and unquenchable sorrow as mothers and

ACTIVATE
• Take a short-term mission trip through a relief organization that specializes in clean water and help build clean-water wells.

• Contact your local and state representatives about the importance of ensuring that all people around the world have access to clean water.

fathers watched their children die, and as they faced choices that they never thought they would have to face. Questions like, *Should we drink the salt water if it is all that will keep us alive for another day? Should we put poison into our bodies?*

The only sound worse than that of a dying child is the sound of *your* dying child.

Some of the most tragic stories I have known about the suffering in Africa are about children. When children do not have clean water to drink, they drink what they can. And when they drink, they contract cholera, typhoid, and malaria. And when they contract stomach viruses that cause diarrhea or vomiting, they are forced to drink more water to combat the dehydration, which only makes them sicker. These children eventually die.

One of the criteria for writing this essay was that I help usher readers into a deeper understanding of why it is important for people to have access to clean water and, in the process of explaining the facts, attempt to give such a human perspective that it would elicit a compassionate response. In the aftermath of Hurricane Katrina, much of my work has been done for me.

Time was of the essence. We could not sit by and let children die. We had to provide the necessary resources immediately. There was a strong sense of urgency in every presidential speech, in every Red Cross report, and in every plea from stranded refugees living in shelters and under highway overpasses. We could feel the injustice; it made us squirm. It gave us something to care about, and everyone pitched in. It was a wonderful display of the good that can well up inside a person in times of crisis.

We take care of our own. Injustices and violations are much larger when they get close to our living rooms, and this tragedy had curled up on the couch next to us. Many people gave what they could to serve those in need. And again, as with the tragedy of September 11 and the collapse of the World Trade Center, Americans mobilized. The majority of help came in the form of money and purchased goods, including bottled water, food, clothing, and medical supplies. It was not difficult to find a way to contribute. Scattered throughout the United States were pickup trucks, semis, and flatbeds ready to haul relief supplies down South.

For anyone familiar with Africa, or the rest of the developing world, the response to the crisis in New Orleans was inspiring—but also troubling.

When we know that nearly 150 children die every hour in Africa from complications surrounding lack of clean water and proper sanitation, and we do not feel the same sense of urgency that we feel when American children begin to die from lack of clean water, we must look at the reasons why. Do we have a hierarchy of life based on the principles of patriotism, or are we provoked by the mandates of Jesus Christ?

These stories are not simply tragic. They are the stories of real injustice. A tragedy would be something that we are helpless to stop. This is injustice because we have the ability to help Africans gain access to clean water. Nearly 80 percent of all deaths in developing countries, more than twenty thousand deaths per day, could be prevented. Information regarding the lack of clean water and proper sanitation shows that it is the poorest and most vulnerable parts of society that have to go without.

How do we reach out to this injustice? How do we change the course of declining access to clean water?

DO SOMETHING

Fund a water project in an African community. Research an organization and write a check. For many people this is the best way to help. Remember, for many communities, the only barrier between clean and unclean water is the inability to pay teams to drill. Through organizations like Lifewater International, Africare, Blood:Water Mission, and WaterAid, you can reach out to Africans in their most basic need. A clean-water well can cost anywhere from $1,000 to $25,000, depending on location, the kind of drilling equipment needed, the depth of the well, and the complexity of the

PRAY

Oh Lord our God, who "satisfies the thirsty and fills the hungry with good things" (Ps. 107:9), please provide those who thirst with pure water to sustain their physical bodies and the bodies of their children and grandchildren for generations to come. And grant to those of us with ready access to clean water the wisdom, fortitude, and financial resources to willingly and joyfully help those without water find access to this vital resource. And finally, Lord, we ask that You quench the thirst of all of our souls with the cool water of the Holy Spirit. Amen.

well system.

Some wells simply need to be repaired. This costs substantially less than constructing a well, but is just as vital.

Blood:Water Mission's 1,000 Wells Project has been funding well projects based on the equation that one U.S. dollar equals clean water for one African for an entire year! Every dollar can make a substantial difference.

Speak up. It is not difficult to understand why a person would need clean water. Many people do not know that there are still people in the world without this very basic staple. Your words can be the catalyst for others to have the privilege of knowing and serving someone in need.

Bring the issue of clean water to your school, church, or business. Many churches have adopted villages and begun the work of developing a long-term relationship. They have sent teams over to get to know the community. In this process, the church has funded well-drilling and other community-development projects.

High-school and college students have a unique ability to mobilize friends and classmates to do fundraising and awareness programs on campus. There is no end to the creative approaches to raising money and awareness for water projects. It has been predicted that by the year 2025, nearly half of the world's population will not have access to clean water or proper sanitation. This prediction is based on current trends and information gathered about the rate of population growth compared to the rate of water-system development. Can we change the course? Yes. We can give life and hope to communities. By God's grace alone, we can walk humbly, serve justice, and give to the least—not simply a cup, but a life full of clean water. It is our move.

DAN HASELTINE is the lead singer for Jars of Clay and founder of Blood: Water Mission, a nonprofit organization combating HIV/AIDS by providing clean-blood and clean-water solutions and developing sustainable, equitable relationships in Africa.

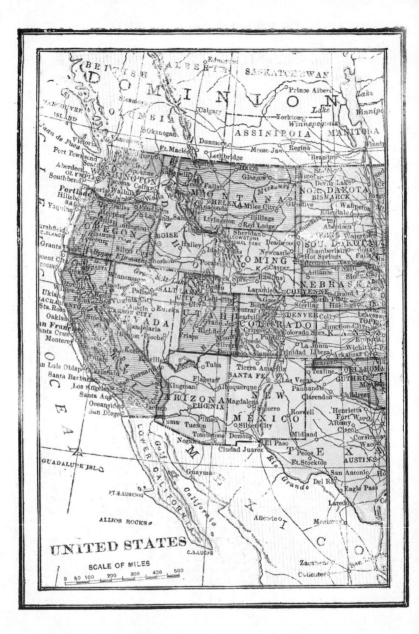

UNITED STATES

SCALE OF MILES

0   50 100   200   300   400   500

CHAPTER TWO

GANG VIOLENCE

BY DOAK BOCK

"THE ULTIMATE WEAKNESS OF VIOLENCE IS THAT IT IS A DESCENDING SPIRAL, BEGETTING THE VERY THING IT SEEKS TO DESTROY ... IN FACT, VIOLENCE MERELY INCREASES HATE ... RETURNING VIOLENCE FOR VIOLENCE MULTIPLIES VIOLENCE, ADDING DEEPER DARKNESS TO A NIGHT ALREADY DEVOID OF STARS." —REV. MARTIN LUTHER KING JR.

Police conduct a raid on an apartment and prepare to force their way through the entrance. On the other side, a twenty-three-year-old man levels a shotgun at the door, cursing and daring them to enter.

A fight breaks out in a penitentiary yard over $3 that was in dispute during a card game earlier in the day. A twenty-two-year-old man is stabbed several times in the chest, stomach, and back with a shank fashioned out of a panhandle.

A sixteen-year-old hides in a church while his former friends surround it and wait patiently for him to come out so they can kill him. After two days of hiding, he is smuggled out of the city in the trunk of the pastor's car.

A twenty-year-old leaves his house one evening and is met by a shotgun blast at point-blank range from behind the bushes in his own yard.

DONATE
Start becoming a regular donor to an anti-gang organization. Donate Christmas gifts through Prison Ministry's Angel Tree Program and other similar programs to children whose parents are in jail. Help pay for a child to attend a special summer camp for at-risk youth.

A group of women catch up to their twenty-three-year-old friend while she is walking down the street alone. They suddenly assault her, beating her and kicking out her two front teeth, and leave her unconscious in the middle of the street.

A seventeen-year-old shows up to a counseling session bruised and beaten, telling his counselor he is relieved and happy that he was able to withstand the head-to-toe pounding he received from his friends.

These events may sound like scenes from a Quentin Tarantino movie, but they all happened to real people who either were or still are gang members I have counseled, worked with, or become friends with over the last twelve years. The amazing thing is that they all survived these encounters that should have claimed their lives. As the cliché goes, truth is stranger than fiction—or in this case, truth is more brutal than fiction. These are common occurrences in the everyday life of a gangster. From the bricks to the sticks, the gospel of the "thug life" has spread and is readily accepted by people from every race, socioeconomic level, and walk of life as they declare allegiance to a trinity of crime, hate, and violence.

THE STARTING POINT

There are as many reasons for joining a gang as there are for staying out of one. There is little doubt gangs are sanctuaries for sociopaths, people for whom violence is enjoyable and fun. Gangs are places where troubled young adults can be accepted and even respected for acting out their violent urges; overall, though, sociopaths make up only a small portion of gang memberships. Most members are, relatively speaking, normal people. So the question should be asked: why do people join gangs, and why are they willing to take part in the violence that goes with it? The answer is complex and varies with each individual, but some general reasons are apparent.

For most it begins in the streets, and for anyone who does not call "the jungle" home, it is their destination—the mecca for any "wannabe," "gonnabe," and "already is" gangbanger. The streets are where everything happens. This "street life" exists in big and small cities, and to a lesser extent in certain areas in the suburbs and even in some of the "quieter" communities. It is a place where a whole different set of rules exists outside of lawful society. These rules work on the premise of "eat or be eaten" and are lived out by people who have few or no restraints, are desperate, and often have little to lose.

The street lifestyle that has been mythologized in music, movies, and videos is right outside the door of many young men and women, beckoning them to follow its path from the moment they are born. The byproducts of this lifestyle are well-known: drug addiction, physical and sexual abuse, prostitution, cruelty, hatred, corrupt morals, violence, and often, early death. Many of the young men and women from the streets live on an island where their whole existence is a few city blocks insulated from the rest of the world. Like the stranded children in *Lord of the Flies*, they have surrendered their civility for ruthlessness and chaos.

> "Violence destroys what it claims to defend: the dignity, the life, the freedom of human beings. Violence is a crime against humanity, for it destroys the very fabric of society."
>
> —POPE JOHN PAUL II

While God holds us all responsible for our own choices, the power of influence cannot be discarded. Jesus recognized the power of influence when He said, "Things that cause people to stumble are bound to come, but woe to anyone through whom they come" (Luke 17:1, TNIV). A ten-year-old may be able to make his own choices, but without proper moral guidance he is likely to make very bad choices, and under the influence of immoral guidance he will make horrific choices. He can learn about the Gandhis and Martin Luther King Jr.s all he wants while he's in school, but at the end of the day, he will go home and see who has the money and power in his neighborhood. Chances are, it isn't his single mom breaking her back to keep the family afloat with two jobs and lots of bills. It's the hustlers and bangers and pimps, the people who prey on others. The young man admires them and daydreams about being like them, picking up on the way things get done in the streets.

Even though much of the flash and bling is often a thin veil of the truth, the illusion is a powerful one to young minds, and without guidance they will not see through the street's siren song until it's too late. A gangster may have no real home and very few belongings, be infected with STDs or other health problems, and have a criminal record longer than a novel. But when he rolls through the neighborhood in an Escalade on dubs with gold chains hanging off his neck, young kids take notice. Usually, once a young person reaches the age of accountability, he has a good handle on the rules of the streets, and doing things any other way literally seems foreign.

Another way to see it is that human beings are followers by nature. If a child sees enough people jumped and beat up as a means to an end, he will soon believe that is an option for him as well, or at the very least feel that that kind of thing is acceptable, even if he understands the consequences. Strong evidence of this kind of learning is evident in domestic abusers—people who often either viewed abuse or were victims of it themselves as children. Without any positives to counter the negativity they see every day, children can quickly become desensitized to violence, increasing their susceptibility to commit violent acts.

RESPECT

One of the biggest draws to gangs is the desire for power and respect. The respect they speak of, however, is not that which most of us understand; it is the allure of power wrapped around a rotten core of fear. Respect in the streets is synonymous with fear—it is not gained through kindness, mutual respect, understanding, or benevolence. It is beaten out of people with fists, drawn out with a gun, or determined by the size of the knot of cash in their pocket. This idea of respect is perhaps the source of much of the aggression and violence expressed by gang members. If someone is challenged, he must respond with force, or he will be perceived as weak—inviting others to take advantage of him. This mentality is borrowed heavily from the penal system, but it is always in effect, even if there is no real threat present. This mentality comes from living a "fight or die" existence. While the person may not physically die, his reputation dies. And on the streets, reputation is as important as actual life. To walk away from a challenge is worse than being beaten down in a fight; to forgive is seen as a weakness, and weakness cannot be tolerated in the jungle.

Many gangsters have difficulties in school because (among other reasons) they carry this code with them and end up getting kicked out for fighting or intimidating other students (usually rival gang members). In the gang member's mind, the eyes of the world are constantly judging him by this twisted idea of respect, and he can never let anything pass without the fear of losing that respect.

The respect one gains in the streets feeds directly into his reputation. Reputation is one of the largest currencies in a gangster's world. It determines how he will be treated and how high he will move up in the gang. Reputation is built by what a person does for the gang, the way he handles himself in the streets, and his loyalty to the group and those above him in rank. Many gangs require initiates to fulfill certain requirements before becoming full-fledged members. These often involve acts of violence that enable the person to demonstrate how "down" he is for the gang. I worked with one young man who recounted that his initiation required him to kill a member of a rival gang. He nervously recalled how he walked up on three members of the opposition shooting dice in an alley, drew his pistol, emptied the clip at them, and ran. Although he was unsure whether or not he actually killed, or even hit, anyone, it was reported that he fulfilled his requirement, and he was welcomed into the gang.

In simple terms, the more fear a person generates, the more respect he gets; the only way to generate more fear than the next guy is to do something even more crazy or violent. It's easy to see how incredibly violent acts can happen when mind-altering drugs, peer pressure, jacked-up emotions, and impulsive blood are mixed with this philosophy.

Being raised in the streets is not the only reason people join gangs, however; gangs are full of people with stable and even good families. They have a fair sense of right and wrong, and have never been abused or abandoned. Some have not grown up in or been influenced (at least directly) by the streets. For these people several logical reasons explain why they would choose to join a gang that will lead them down the road of violence.

THRILLS

One of the most obvious reasons a person joins a gang is for the sheer thrill of gang life. Drugs, sex, guns, fighting, stealing, running from the police—gangs are an adrenaline amusement park for unchecked testosterone. Thrill-seeking is a common adolescent and young-adult pastime, where doing "crazy" things is seen as a somewhat normal activity. The problem is, a gangster's baseline of what's "crazy" is much higher than other people's, and his willingness to take bigger risks is greater. Young males in particular are full of aggressive tendencies pushing to be released, and for many, fighting is not an unusual pastime, whether they are in gangs or not. The only difference is that someone in a gang has easier access to guns and other weapons—and many more reasons to fight.

There comes a time, however, when this life catches up to them. Such a risky, unfettered lifestyle often leads to addiction, health problems, and, of course, legal trouble. There are not too many forty-year-old active gangbangers out there, and you can bet they're not out on the street mixing it up—they're calling the shots and letting the young bucks take all the risks. Sadly, many young men and women find out too late that this is not the way God meant for them to live their lives.

Thrills and kicks are a big reason the wannabes and false flaggers, usually suburban or rural youth who have had the gangster life exported to them via the media, want to join gangs. However, recruiting by some gangs has sprouted up in the past few decades, with a few members moving to areas outside of the city to begin charter memberships to instruct willing and eager youth about the ways of the gang. More often than not, these youngsters join with MTV visions running through their heads of being "playas" and "ballas," only to end up getting much more than they bargained for—sooner or later they will be called upon to do something illegal, and likely violent, in the name of the gang. Very few, if any, will say no, due either to peer pressure or fear for their own safety.

PROPAGANDA

Like most rational people who commit irrational acts, there is usually a heavy dose of propaganda involved. While not as irrational as terror organizations, gangs use many of the same techniques terrorists use to enlist people to commit violence. Many gang recruits are young boys with family troubles and few friends. They desire a father figure, or seek meaning or purpose, or perhaps are disillusioned with what society has to offer, and they are given assurance by the organization that their families will be taken care of in their absence (i.e., if they are locked up). They are then indoctrinated with the gang's philosophy, which can involve a kind of brainwashing to create unquestioned loyalty to the group. The rival gangs are demonized and opposition members dehumanized, and the initiates are told of past attacks and disrespect from the opposition. All of this creates a condition in the young and impressionable, so that when they see a rival gang member, there is no hesitation to react aggressively. Many times a banger will commit violence against a rival without ever knowing who the person is or ever having been personally wronged by him— he is simply "the enemy." One fifteen-year-old recounted to me how he had shot at several boys who had walked down his street one night. I asked if he knew any of them, and he replied, "No, but I thought I saw one of them throw up a (rival) hand sign," as if that was reason enough.

EDUCATE
Learn about gangs and what causes young people to gravitate toward them, then educate others and work to dispel myths about gangs and gang violence.

Many gangs also have what they call literature, or a "lit," which plays a major role in the indoctrination of the young person. It is a written document containing the gang's charter, bylaws, rules, and code of conduct. It usually contains heavy doses of emotionally charged statements and philosophies designed to instill pride for the gang and hatred for the opposition. Initiates are required to know their lit by heart and are tested on it before they are accepted into the gang. Failure to know the lit results in varying degrees of discipline, from a punch in the face to a timed beating against a wall by several gang members.

But just like any kind of propaganda, once the truth is revealed, the emotions connected to it fall away, and with them the will to do violence. I have seen rival members become friends in places outside of the influence of the gangs and the streets, such as in drug rehabs, outreach programs, or church, once they get to know each other and realize that there is a higher calling in life than hatred and revenge.

SELF-PRESERVATION

Many children who are not part of the pack are the prey. Eleven- and twelve-year-olds can expect to be recruited by gangs with the promise that they will watch the youngsters' backs and take care of anyone who messes with them. And the gangs deliver on that promise.

Many gangs were originally formed along racial lines. In cities with cultural and racial tension, joining a gang may be the safest thing a person can do for himself and his family. For many, it may be an act of national or racial pride. Gangbanging due to racial division is particularly true in the prison system, especially west of the Mississippi River. Even if someone is not an active member of a gang, when he enters the prison system, his only hope of survival is to join the gang with members from his own race. There are few things as emotionally explosive as race, and it should be no surprise that it is used among the gangs to generate violence.

Perhaps not as racially motivated are territorial claims to specific neighborhoods or areas. This was the main source for gangbanging in the '60s and '70s. As one old-timer put it, "It wasn't about money back then; it was about the turf." Keeping the opposition out of the gang's neighborhood was of primary importance. This mutated form of community pride would later develop into struggles over space to sell drugs in the '80s and '90s.

Self-preservation is also one of the main reasons people do

not leave gangs—if they do, they will be open game for their old adversaries, who don't care if they've left the game or not. I was told by one young man that after he quit his gang, he had to be on constant watch because he was now "alone." As hard as he tried to avoid rival gang members, they soon caught wind of his decision and harassed him routinely at school. Within a matter of days, a car full of rival gang members rolled by and opened fire on him as he walked home from school. Luckily they missed. He, of course, knew he would face this before he quit his gang, but he went through with it

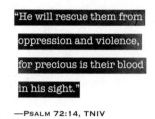

"He will rescue them from oppression and violence, for precious is their blood in his sight."

—Psalm 72:14, TNIV

because he knew it was the right thing to do. He was fifteen at the time. No one can say these young men and women lack courage.

Another point to consider is that many gangsters who leave their gang are not only fresh meat for the opposition, but also targets for their own gang, which may put an "SOS" or "Shoot on Sight" order out on them. This simply means if any of the old gang's associates see him, they are to attack him, whether it be by shooting, stabbing, or beating. This is the penalty for many who choose to leave their gang. In these cases the person who has left the gang has not only lost any protection he once had from his original enemies, he has now doubled his enemies in the process.

SOLUTIONS

So what can be done? Can any of these young men and women be saved from the thug life? Can the streets be undone, or is the saying true—"You can't beat the streets; the streets will always beat you"? Is it possible to bring a gangster back?

There is hope, and many have been transformed from the life of violence. Through the redemptive power of Jesus Christ and God's awesome grace, even the most hard-core gangster can change. "Therefore, if anyone is in Christ, he is a new creation; the old has gone, the new has come!" (2 Cor. 5:17, NIV). Often the support of one or two good people can make a difference in the life of a young person making that fateful decision to join or desert a gang.

You may be the furthest thing from a thug, but you can still make a difference. One simple thing we can all do is make an effort to help these people feel welcome in our churches. Too often, even in the cities and urban areas they call home, these youth are ignored or made to feel unwelcome in church because of the way people perceive them. I am not suggesting you try to convince your pastor to wear big platinum chains, sag his pants, and get some gold teeth; I am simply suggesting we be non-judgmental of the way they dress and talk. The body of Christ has plenty of room for variety; they should not be excluded simply because their ways are different.

ACTIVATE

Mentor a troubled youth, especially one whose mother or father is in jail for gang-related activity or who has been or is in a gang.

A good point to remember is that many gangsters are religious, and some gangs have pseudo-religious components in their makeup. For example, some believe that God has ordained them to protect their "nation" (the gang) and/or neighborhood through violence; some even have specific prayers to God for their gang. The point is that many of these young men and women have the desire for faith, and they are only waiting for someone to show them true faith. Though they claim to be religious, they often do not know much about Christianity, and any opportunity to bring them the Truth is a step in the right direction.

With gangsters, the process toward salvation is often a seed-planting exercise. They are often resistant or suspicious of anyone talking "at" them or giving them a "sales pitch," but if we gently plant seeds, perhaps by inviting them to share their opinion about morals or beliefs about God and then humbly sharing our own views, we give them something to think about on their own, and invariably they will come back with more questions. Most—if not all—gangsters are keenly aware that what they are doing is wrong, and learning that God will forgive them and wipe their slate clean can be an extraordinary experience for them.

Becoming a mentor is an excellent preventive measure to keep young children from being drawn into gangs and the street lifestyle. In some cities there are two- or three-year wait lists for children who want a mentor. One person's positive influence and caring can have an impact in the life of a young person who has few or no role models. The simple act of removing a child from his negative neighborhood for a few hours each week and showing him that there is more in the world than the few blocks that make up his neighborhood can have powerful results.

Something else that has been successful is participation in the Angel Tree Program. It involves church members pooling and selecting names of incarcerated persons with families and buying their children presents at Christmastime. Many gangbangers are very devoted to family, and this can be a huge leverage with them. It only takes one act of kindness to make a gangster who is a parent in jail realize that there is something more than a dog-eat-dog world out there, and gratitude often leads the person back to the church

PRAY

Lord, in this age of Individualism and loneliness, we all need strong, healthy families and communities more than ever. We pray that You help us keep Your precious children, who have a longing for communal support, from joining dangerous and destructive gangs; instead, draw them into the loving arms of those who would nurture them as the tender flowers that they are, rather than suffocate them with the weeds of lies, addiction, and crime. Help us, who care so deeply for children and young adults, to step up to the important task of mentoring troubled youth, building strong communities centered on love. Amen.

responsible for the kind act. I have witnessed an entire gang outreach ministry sprout from this kind of program.

Similarly, simply writing to a prisoner is a great opportunity to reach someone involved in a gang. While they are banging, most gangsters will proclaim loyalty to their boys and maybe even pledge their life to the gang, but when they end up in jail, it is rare if they receive even one letter from fellow members. Imprisonment is a prime time to reach these young men and women because they will begin to question their decisions and think about what they have become and where they want to go in life. A letter once a month can help them answer their questions and can begin to build a bridge for the Holy Spirit to cross. You don't have to know all the street lingo—or anything at all about gangs—to care, and that is what reaches them the most—the knowledge that someone cares about them when it seems no one else does.

For those who would like to become more involved, a prison ministry is a good way to reach gangsters who are locked up. Holding Bible studies for prisoners or offering assistance with GED or other educational studies may be possible in some places.

If you would like to work directly with young men and women involved in gangs or the street lifestyle but lack experience, try volunteering in urban ministries to get your feet wet.

If you still feel wary about becoming directly involved with urban/gang youth, you can financially support one of the various gang or urban youth ministries in your city or county. Often these programs struggle with finding places to meet, getting volunteers to help out, and obtaining funds to finance outings or buy equipment for their programs.

And, of course, the most deeply personal and effective thing you can do is pray. Praying for the young men and women from the streets, stuck in the streets, unwilling to leave the streets, who are consumed by anger, addiction, greed, and spiritual blindness, is a simple, anonymous act that carries eternal implications. "The prayer of a righteous man is powerful and effective" (James 5:16, TNIV).

DOAK BOCK is an adolescent-substance-abuse counselor and outreach worker for Gateway Foundation in Lake Villa, Illinois, and works with Lake County Gang Outreach as editor of publications. He leads a nomadic life, traveling frequently between southeastern Wisconsin and northeastern Illinois looking for good places to mountain-bike and kayak.

CHINESE EMPIRE

SCALE OF MILES

CHINA SEA

CHAPTER THREE

WOMEN'S RIGHTS

BY MARIE SMITH

"CAUTIOUS, CAREFUL PEOPLE, ALWAYS
CASTING ABOUT TO PRESERVE THEIR
REPUTATION AND SOCIAL STANDING, NEVER
CAN BRING ABOUT A REFORM. THOSE WHO
ARE REALLY IN EARNEST MUST BE WILLING
TO BE ANYTHING OR NOTHING IN THE WORLD'S
ESTIMATION." —SUSAN B. ANTHONY

In a small town in rural China, government officials and others came for Hu Shuye. She describes thirty to forty people coming to her home and dragging her away for an abortion. She had broken the law by becoming pregnant again, a violation of the government-mandated "one child per couple" policy. Her penalty was forced abortion when she was six months pregnant, followed in a few months by forced sterilization.[1]

Blond-haired, blue-eyed Tanya stands out in the dark-haired

group of sex-trafficking victims in Greece. She came to Athens to work as a waitress, desperate to provide her two daughters back in Russia with the basic necessities of life. She had accepted the job offer, thinking she would work for two years and then return home. But there was no waitressing job, no restaurant—only a brothel where she was forced to sacrifice her body many times a day—or else. Tanya was told her daughters would be hurt and even killed if she tried to escape.[2]

Goma, a wife and mother in Nepal, works from before the sun rises until after it sets, gathering grasses for the hungry water buffalo, hulling and pounding rice, tending the small fields with primitive equipment, and endlessly preparing food over a fire pit. She has a nagging cough from the smoke. She can neither read nor write and has never traveled outside her small mountain village. She birthed her three children alone.

Millions of women around the world, women like Hu Shuye, Tanya, and Goma, are largely invisible in their struggle for survival, particularly in developing countries. We may catch glimpses—through photographs, news stories, documentaries, perhaps our own travels—but most women remain unseen.

Each of these unseen women is unique. As a group, however, their unmet needs are tragically similar. In the diverse realms of women's lives—economic, social, political, physical, emotional, educational, spiritual—their basic needs are not met. Their basic human rights are not secured. Their well-being is neither protected nor promoted.

These unseen women embody what is called the "feminization of poverty." Many more women than men live in extreme poverty, struggling to survive on less than $1 a day. Women in Africa and Asia walk more than three miles a day to get clean water. African women, more than men, work as subsistence farmers, tilling the dry and poor soil. Women are often denied access to training for better-paying jobs. They are victims of gender-based violence and abuse. Basic resources for women, including nutrition, sanitation, and health care, are woefully lacking.[3]

Improving the lives of unseen women calls for dramatic, decisive, and sustained action. In short, what is needed is nothing less than a revolution that results in lasting change. As is the nature of social transformations, such change seems impossible—until it happens.

DONATE
Make a donation to an organization that helps ensure basic human rights to women. Donate packages of new women's underwear to a rape crisis center for women returning home from the hospital after being raped.

In the United States, American women led such a revolution more than 150 years ago, when they faced conditions similar to those experienced by women in developing countries today. Like so many women in various nations today, they labored long and hard hours in deplorable conditions. Women could not own or inherit land or property. They could not vote. They were denied custody of their children if they divorced or, in some cases, if they were widowed. They were limited in education and could not go to college. Certain jobs and professions were off limits. Women were abused sexually, and the crimes often went unpunished. Women died in childbirth, and half their children died before age five.

The movement for women's rights in the United States began to accelerate in 1876, when Susan B. Anthony, now one of the best-known early American feminists, began publishing a newsletter called *The Revolution*. She, Elizabeth Cady Stanton, and other leaders of this revolution were proper ladies who rocked their world with a radical message: women had rights equal to those of men, and they should be guaranteed those rights by law.

The rights sought by these early American feminists are still widely relevant: women deserved equal pay for equal work; qualified women should be able to work in traditionally male jobs; women should be able to attend college and pursue careers in professions like medicine or law; women should be able to divorce an abusive husband. Above all else, women should have the right to vote. The early American feminists recognized that if women were to have any influence in their world and participate as full citizens, they must be able to vote in local and national elections. These rights are still not secured for many women across the globe. Women's right to vote, for example, is still being advanced and resisted in some countries, notably in the Persian Gulf region.

> "Loneliness and the feeling of being unwanted is the most terrible poverty."
>
> —MOTHER TERESA

Of great significance is that these feminists who successfully expanded the rights of women also established legal protections from abortion for women and children. Anthony described abortion in *The Revolution* as "child murder" and "infanticide."[4]

The very laws the early American feminists fought for—to protect women and children from abortion—were the ones destroyed by the Supreme Court decisions in 1973 (Roe v. Wade and Doe v. Bolton), which legalized abortion on demand for all nine months of pregnancy.

Abortion-rights feminists of the 1960s and 1970s rejected the original feminist principles of nondiscrimination, nonviolence, and justice for all in their push to legalize abortion. Abortion discriminates against a class of people due to their size (small) and location (womb). It inflicts violence that destroys the child and may cause physical, emotional, and spiritual harm to the woman. Finally, abortion denies justice to the unborn child whose life is ended—and to the woman whose real needs go unmet.

Women's real needs are clear. According to the Alan Guttmacher Institute, the research arm of Planned Parenthood, women today have abortions for two primary reasons: lack of financial resources and lack of emotional support.[5]

The early American feminists did not see abortion as a solution to a woman's problems and needs. Abortion was viewed as violence, as exploitation, and as part of the problem. It was seen, in fact, as a barrier to women's rights and full equality. Alice Paul, author of the Equal Rights Amendment (ERA), stated simply: "Abortion is the ultimate exploitation of women."[6] Today, Feminists for Life lives the legacy of our feminist foremothers as we advocate for lasting solutions to meet the needs of women. It is dedicated to systematically eliminating the root causes that drive women to abortion through holistic, woman-centered solutions.

Unfortunately, abortion is promoted internationally as a reproductive right and as a necessity for women's lives and health. It is falsely portrayed as safe. In reality, abortion is a reflection that governments and societies have failed to meet the needs of women. Women deserve better than abortion, no matter where they live.

Acceptance of abortion as a solution means society no longer has to take pregnancy seriously and meet the real needs of women. This is what the early American feminists understood—and what continues to motivate Feminists for Life today.

What women want and need is full participation as citizens, equal access to resources and opportunities, and enforced legal protection against discrimination, violence, and oppression. The emphasis must be on addressing root causes and promoting lasting solutions, from prevention to practical resources. The basic rights of women must be secured and maintained.

RIGHT TO EDUCATION

Education is the most empowering choice for any woman's future. It is foremost among the solutions to the increasing "feminization of poverty." Two-thirds of the world's illiterate people are female, and these women are left with very few options to create decent lives for themselves.[7]

Sadly, some parents and community leaders do not see compelling reasons to invest in education for girls. When a family's resources are limited, they may sacrifice to send the sons to school, but not the daughters. The girls stay home, help their mothers, and prepare to join generations of women trapped in poverty.

The opportunity and ability to attend school are vital for girls. Education protects a girl by preparing her for productive adulthood. It helps to protect her from the lure of traffickers and prepares her for a future of promise.

Women who have had the benefit of education have more opportunities to make a living wage, receive respect, and provide community leadership. Their health is better, resulting in safer pregnancies and deliveries and stronger, healthier children. They can make more informed decisions for themselves and their children.

RIGHT TO ECONOMIC EMPOWERMENT

Economic empowerment, including access to vocational and skill training and job opportunities, is necessary for women. Roseline in Ethiopia, rescued from the grip of sex trafficking, has learned to make sandals and other goods from leather. She proudly sells these and is now self-employed—an important option for women.

Microcredit loans are a remarkable means to provide a woman with the ability to earn a sustainable income to feed her family and meet basic needs. Even very small loans can transform women's lives. Many microcredit programs also bring women together to support one another and begin to build social capital in their villages.

In Sri Lanka, Blanca received a small loan of $35 to purchase ingredients to make and sell sweets. Her success enabled her to open a kiosk to sell additional items as well. She is now able to put food on the table, educate her children, and afford health care. She has respect for herself, and others in the community look to her for leadership. This gives her new opportunities for political involvement and the chance to advocate for changes that will create even broader benefits.

EDUCATE
Read *Real Choices* by Frederica Mathewes-Green, a book that thoughtfully addresses the realities of abortion. Learn whatever you can about the facts surrounding rape, domestic violence, crisis pregnancy, and abortion. Learn about the different ways women continue to be mistreated around the world and share what you learn with other concerned citizens.

Often a woman is the sole wage earner for her family. She may have been widowed or abandoned by the father of her children, or she may have a husband or partner who cannot work. She must earn a living wage that can sustain her family. Yet, for example, the average daily wage for a service worker in El Salvador is $5.28 a day.[8] A woman working in a fast-food franchise like Pizza Hut or KFC in San Salvador would have to work an entire day to afford one meal from the U.S.-priced menu.

RIGHT TO BE PROTECTED FROM ABUSE

Acts of violence, exploitation, and abuse against women and girls are rampant in many regions of the world. Trafficking and rape, domestic violence, and enslavement of girls as child soldiers are among the more prevalent abuses.

TRAFFICKING

Terms like *sex trafficking*, *involuntary servitude*, *debt bondage*, *coercion*, and *commercial sex acts* are all part of the horrific picture of trafficking. Trafficking women and children across borders for prostitution and forced labor ruins 600,000 to 800,000 lives a year, especially in Eastern Europe and Southeast Asia. When the number of trafficking victims within countries like India are included, the total can reach into the millions.[9]

Trafficking reduces women and children to commodities that are bought and sold, used and abused. Those who abuse trafficked women and children include men from Western countries such as the United States and the United Kingdom who visit primarily Asian nations as "sex tourists." The accessibility and anonymity of the Internet enables them to view the faces and bodies of young girls, some as young as six, and make arrangements to conduct "business" abusing these young victims. Under the U.S. Protect Act, sex tourism is illegal, and the FBI and Department of Justice are both tracking and prosecuting abusers.

The profit must be taken out of trafficking at all levels—from the desperate relatives who sell young girls from their own families to the traffickers and those who benefit at the expense of women and children. The landmark Trafficking Victims Protection Act of 2000 and its reauthorization are enabling U.S. federal district attorneys to prosecute traffickers in increasing numbers.

RAPE

Women suffer greatly from rape, especially in war-torn regions and as internally displaced persons (IDPs) seeking a home. The increased vulnerability of women in these situations makes them easier targets for rapists. Furthermore, rape is used as a weapon of war. In a host of recent conflicts—from Bosnia-Herzegovina to Darfur in western Sudan—rape has been used to violate, humiliate, and destroy the enemy.

Even those who are meant to protect vulnerable groups in conflict situations have abused women. Some United Nations' peacekeeping troops, for example, have victimized women in refugee camps in Congo and have been complicit in sex trafficking in Kosovo.[10] Women need security and have a right to be protected. The United Nations and all governments must hold their soldiers accountable for their actions and render appropriate punishment.

VIOLENCE IN THE HOME

Domestic abuse harms millions of women throughout the world, many of whom have little legal power to protect themselves and their children. Laws on domestic violence are needed to give all women legal recourse to escape violent situations without being further victimized by loss of child custody or property.

Shelters must be provided for women and children. No woman anywhere should have to live in fear of being abused in her own home. No young girl should have to fear that a male family member or family friend will rape her while she sleeps.

In the United States there is a hotline for women experiencing domestic abuse, the National Domestic Violence Hotline (NDVH), 1-800-799-SAFE. It provides essential information and connections with people who are ready to help battered women and their children escape to safety. Women in other countries often do not have the option to leave.

> "There is neither Jew nor Gentile, neither slave nor free, neither male nor female, for you are all one in Christ Jesus."
> —GALATIANS 3:28, TNIV

Tragically, homicide is a leading cause of death for pregnant women in the United States. According to an article in the *Washington Post* on February 23, 2005, the Centers for Disease Control and Prevention (CDC) reports that homicide ranks second after auto accidents for causing violent death to pregnant women and new mothers. It shows a troubling number of pregnant women and new mothers are being killed by gunfire, stabbing, and physical assault with other weapons. One of the researchers was quoted as saying, "There is a phenomenon going on out there, and we don't understand it yet."[11]

While researchers examine the contributing factors in order to prevent further violence against pregnant women, we must simultaneously reach out to rescue the victims and help the abusers stop the violence—always providing legal protection for mothers and children. Assaulting a pregnant woman to cause an abortion is violence upon violence.

CHILD SOLDIERS

Girls and boys in places like northern Uganda, Congo, and Sudan are kidnapped by armies, insurgents, terrorist groups, and gangs and forced into brutal roles as child soldiers. They must kill or be killed. These victims are violently abused in all ways and forced to commit acts of unspeakable brutality.

The phenomenon of child soldiering is a growing crisis in a number of African and Asian countries and occurs in the Americas, Eurasia, and the Middle East as well. Amnesty International reports, "Although research suggests that 300,000 child soldiers are exploited in over thirty conflicts around the world, in fact, no one knows the real number."[12]

Children's lives are destroyed and tormented. Mary, a sixteen-year-old demobilized child soldier in central Africa, remembers: "I feel so bad about the things that I did. It disturbs me so much that I inflicted death on other people ... I still dream about the boy from my village whom I killed."[13]

RIGHTS DENIED BY CULTURAL PRACTICES

A number of cultural practices devalue female lives and cause unimaginable suffering—from acid burnings and so-called honor killings to female genital mutilation to rapes of young girls in the false belief that it will cure the rapist's HIV/AIDS. It is the responsibility of governments to ensure that all citizens are protected from violent cultural practices.

In some African countries the tradition of early marriage is devastating to girls. Instead of attending school, many young girls marry and bear children. But their underdeveloped bodies cannot bear the strain of delivery. Without skilled midwives and access to modern obstetrical care for cesarean-section deliveries, a disabling health condition known as obstetric fistula can result.

In countries like India and China, where there is a strong

43

ACTIVATE

• Become a rape crisis or crisis pregnancy counselor.

• Be willing to adopt a child that might otherwise be aborted or offer to feed, clothe, shelter, and nurture a young unwed mother and her child.

• Volunteer at your local shelter for battered women and children.

• Take a short-term mission trip with an organization that ministers to the needs of mistreated and abused women around the globe.

• Be ready to help a victim of domestic abuse by learning the signs of abuse, the steps of preparation for a woman to escape an abusive situation, and your local shelter's address and phone number—memorize the National Domestic Violence Hotline: (800) 799-SAFE.

cultural preference for male children, girls are targeted for death by sex-selective abortion, infanticide, or abandonment after birth.

India is facing a looming population imbalance as sex-selective abortions continue to eliminate baby girls, even though the practice is illegal. An oppressive dowry system fuels the problem. A son is expected to financially support his parents and his wife. A daughter is seen as an expensive burden, as she will require a dowry in order to marry and provide little value to her family once married.

Regarding China, the U.S. State Department's Country Report on Human Rights Practices 2003 states, "Female infanticide, sex-selective abortions, and the abandonment and neglect of baby girls remained problems due to the traditional preference for sons and the birth limitation policy."[14]

In London's *Guardian* newspaper, Li Weixiong, a population consultant for the People's Republic of China, speaks frankly about the demographic crisis facing China as the preference for boys has created a critical shortage of female babies. "Such serious gender disproportion poses a major threat to the healthy, harmonious and sustainable growth of the nation's population and would trigger such crimes and social problems as abduction of women and prostitution."[15]

Chinese cultural practices that limit women and force them into subservient positions also contribute to a suicide rate reported to be five times that of any other country. It is estimated that at least five hundred Chinese women daily are taking their own lives. According to the State Department report, "Violence against women and girls, discrimination in education and employment, the traditional preference for male children, the country's birth limitation policies, and other societal factors contributed to the especially high female suicide rate."

RIGHT TO HEALTH CARE

Holistic health care is a woman's right and should be available to all women. Prenatal care, safe and sanitary assisted delivery, postpartum care, emergency services, immunizations, and disease prevention and treatment, especially for the HIV/AIDS pandemic, will save women's lives. This must be a priority of governments.

Women are dying not because they need abortion, as abortion advocates claim, but because they need access to health care. Women in developing countries need a nutritional diet and supplements for deficiencies like anemia. They are desperate for the prevention and treatment of killer diseases like malaria, tuberculosis, and HIV/AIDS.

While some assert that large numbers of women are dying from illegal abortion, the World Health Organization acknowledges that data on abortion are scarce and subject to substantial error. The numbers cited are most often based on estimates from groups

PRAY

Lord, You who lovingly fashioned the first woman, called a young virgin to bear and nurture Your only begotten Son, raised up a young girl from death, spoke with love and forgiveness to the Samaritan woman at the well, appeared first to Your women disciples after You rose from the dead, and have called both men and women to be numbered among the saints, we pray that you will have mercy upon all those women around the world who are abused, objectified, enslaved, tortured, belittled, and mistreated. And we pray that all women be lifted up and honored as human beings equal of Your love, mercy, and salvation and the love and respect of their fellow humans. Amen.

promoting an abortion agenda.

A similar tactic was instrumental in securing support for legalized abortion in the United States in the 1970s. Abortion provider Dr. Bernard Nathanson, who later became pro-life, states in his book *Aborting America* that he and another man, Lawrence Lader, invented the numbers of women dying from illegal abortions at that time.

Nathanson admitted that he, Lader, and the abortion advocacy group NARAL (the National Association to Repeal the Abortion Laws) lied about the number of women they claimed were killed by illegal abortion, as part of their successful strategy to push for legalizing abortion in the United States: "It was always five thousand to ten thousand deaths a year. I confess that I knew the figures were totally false ... but in the 'morality' of our revolution, it was a useful figure, widely accepted."[16]

In fact, in 1972, the year before abortion was legalized, the CDC reported that forty-one women had died due to illegal abortion.[17] While any death from abortion is a tragedy, clearly there were not thousands, as abortion advocates claimed.

RIGHT TO REPRODUCTIVE HEALTH

All women need adequate health care, including trained medical care for gynecological and obstetrical concerns. Reproductive health cannot be separated from women's health in general.

Abortion, by any definition, is not "health care." It is not part of "reproductive health." Health care should be life-affirming; it should not end the life of one patient and potentially injure the other.

Efforts in Africa must focus on prevention and treatment of fistula. This disabling disorder resulting from an obstructed delivery leaves a woman with such severe tissue damage that she is unable to control her body's discharges from bowel and bladder. If it is not repaired, she lives an agonizing life. She may be shunned by her family because of the offensive smell and complications. She may also suffer the loss of her child, often the only child she will ever have.

It is estimated that more than two million women live with fistula, a preventable condition that, if contracted, can be treated with surgery. Traditional birth attendants need training in modern obstetric care, learning to spot possible birth complications before labor begins and seek help at hospitals. More fistula hospitals are needed to restore women to life and health.

The terms "reproductive health" and "reproductive health care services" are at the center of abortion debates at the United Nations. These terms can be code for "abortion" and hinder efforts to provide women with the genuine reproductive health care they need and deserve.

RIGHTS FOR DISABLED
AND ELDERLY WOMEN

Many nations, especially in Europe, are facing a "birth dearth" after years of abortion on demand. Birth rates are low, resulting in fewer workers to help meet the needs of an aging population. There is growing concern that this may fuel attempts to legalize euthanasia in countries where it is currently illegal.

In the Netherlands, legislation is moving toward legalizing euthanasia and assisted suicide for elderly and infirm adults and even children as young as twelve, and new laws have been passed allowing "infant euthanasia" when a baby with disabilities is born. ABC News reported that a doctor and his medical team at Groningen Hospital ended the lives of four babies born with spina bifida.[18]

Disability-rights activists strongly object to this proposed legislation and raise concerns about the rights of disabled women. They are right to be concerned. Today women are pressured to sacrifice their children to abortion; tomorrow will they be pressured to sacrifice themselves to euthanasia?

WOMEN DESERVE BETTER

There are great challenges to the quality and dignity of women's lives throughout the world. Too many women are living in extreme poverty; denied access to health care, education, and economic opportunities; forced to give birth in dangerous conditions; abused by husbands and others; trafficked for sex; dying from AIDS and other diseases; and not allowed to vote. Yet with sustained commitment and support, a revolution of change can transform the lives of women worldwide.

Life-affirming programs must be supported with government policies, personal commitments of time and effort, and financial investment to improve women's lives. Contributions to direct service organizations like World Vision and Catholic Relief Services can truly bring about a revolution of change in individual lives.

The United States Congress, the White House, and the United Nations need to hear a pro-woman, pro-child message as they consider legislation affecting international-aid programs.

Your voice, advocating respect and dignity for women, can start a revolution of change in your own backyard. Local transformations, in place after place, can help to eliminate violence, abuse, and exploitation across the world.

In 1848, at the Seneca Falls Convention, American women began a successful revolution that advanced women's rights while protecting women and children from abortion. It was never an easy road, yet, as Susan B. Anthony declared, "Failure is impossible."

We must do all we can to meet the urgent needs of women with life-affirming solutions and to ensure their rights with life-protecting actions. Your efforts do make a difference.

MARIE SMITH is the international director for Feminists for Life (FFL), a nonsectarian, nonpartisan grassroots organization that seeks equality for all human beings and champions the needs of women around the world. She began her pro-woman, pro-life activism in college and has expanded her advocacy worldwide. She represents FFL at the United Nations and travels internationally to discuss the global needs of women with government officials and other leaders.

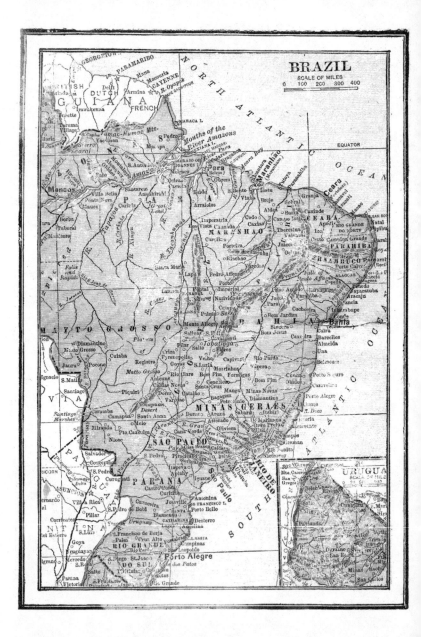

BRAZIL

SCALE OF MILES
0   100   200   300   400

FAIR TRADE

BY JOE CURNOW

"DISTANCE DOES NOT DECIDE WHO IS YOUR
BROTHER AND WHO IS NOT. THE CHURCH IS
GOING TO HAVE TO BECOME THE CONSCIENCE
OF THE FREE MARKET IF IT'S TO HAVE ANY
MEANING IN THIS WORLD—AND STOP BEING
ITS APOLOGIST." —BONO

I learned how to roast coffee over a wood stove in a two-room mud house. On the western border of a coffee plantation between Pacotí and Guaramiranga in northeastern Brazil, I sat with Andrea, sorting and stirring the beans. Though Andrea was only a year older than me, at twenty-one her life was dramatically different from anything I would ever know. When her husband could find work, it was in the coffee fields for meager wages. She stayed home and cared for their three malnourished children. In the hours I spent in their house roasting beans, I learned more about coffee, exploitation, and life than in all of my classes during my semester studying abroad.

A year later, I returned to Brazil to conduct research for my honors thesis. This time, though, instead of living on a coffee plantation, I lived on a Fair Trade coffee cooperative in Poço Fundo, Minas Gerais. I roasted coffee beans over a gas stove in cement-block houses replete with electricity, running water, and televisions. Surprisingly, the most significant difference between the two coffee communities was not in the quality of life; it was in the community empowerment. In Poço Fundo, the community was vibrant, organized into a democratic cooperative and mobilized around community development. Members of the cooperative were family farmers who owned their own small plots of land, were able to feed their children, and dreamed of a future where they could send their children to college.

I spent months studying the effects of Fair Trade certification on the Poço Fundo community and returned to the United States even more convinced of the potential of the Fair Trade movement to revolutionize the dominant paradigm of development and trade.

COFFEE CRISIS

In my time in Brazil, both on the coffee cooperative and on the plantation, I quickly learned that coffee is much more than the steaming beverage many people enjoy each morning. It is the primary source of income for more than twenty-five million coffee producers around the globe.[1]

Since 1989, the international coffee market has collapsed. Changing price structures within the commodity chain, neoliberal policy reforms, the dissolution of the International Coffee Agreement (ICA), and a worldwide coffee glut have devastated the coffee market. The ICA was "a set of international agreements that set production and consumption quotas and governed quality standards from 1969 to 1989."[2] Through the ICA, producing and consuming countries set predetermined supply levels through export quotas with the goal of keeping coffee supplies and prices stable. In 1989, the United States left the International Coffee Organization. Losing the number-one coffee-consuming country caused the price floors to collapse, and the rigidly controlled market was replaced almost overnight by an unregulated one.

DONATE
Make a donation to a Fair Trade organization or shop regularly at a local Fair Trade shop.

In the early 1990s coffee prices soared, but as a result of overproduction and corporate behavior, the per-sack prices have fallen—by almost 50 percent—since 2000. Today the owners of coffee farms are maintaining their land at a deficit. Many are stopping coffee production, laying off workers, and attempting to sell their land. Market forces have created an environment that challenges coffee producers, and coffee corporations have exacerbated the situation. Despite annual profit increases for the world's largest coffee processors, prices paid to farmers have fallen to a thirty-year low—the real price has fallen to 20 percent of what it was in 1960.[3] Where producers once captured 55 percent of the coffee dollar, they now earn less than 22 percent.[4] In real terms, producers now receive $.60 per pound, compared to the $1.80 they earned five years ago.[5]

Coffee-producing communities have felt the consequences acutely. Hunger and poverty have become the norm. Both the United Nations World Food Programme and the United States

Agency for International Development have cited falling coffee prices as a cause of poverty and food insecurity. In some areas, the low prices that farmers receive for their coffee result in "pre-starvation." The diminished prices not only result in reduced purchasing, but also limit the family's ability to send children to school and pay for desperately needed health care. Unable to pay school fees or needing additional labor, families frequently require their children (most often girls) to stop attending primary school, and they rarely return. Families rapidly accumulate debt and have little or no recourse for paying it off. Banks and governments foreclose on properties; coffee producers lose their land and are forced to move to urban centers or emigrate. Unsustainable prices have left coffee-producing communities with few options for survival.

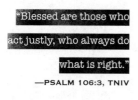

"Blessed are those who act justly, who always do what is right."
—PSALM 106:3, TNIV

While the coffee crisis has affected 125 million people around the world, it is by no means the only agricultural good that is vulnerable to unfair trade rules and a volatile world market. Rice, cotton, sugar, tea, bananas, cacao, and hundreds of other products are impacted as well. Each of these products is affected differently, but all of the communities that produce these goods desperately need sustainable, living-wage alternatives.

WHAT IS FAIR TRADE?

According to the Fairtrade Labelling Organization International (FLO), Fair Trade is an alternative approach to conventional international trade. It is a trading partnership aimed at obtaining sustainable development for excluded and disadvantaged producers through provision of better trading conditions. By creating direct relationships between producers and buyers, producers can get a better price and buyers are guaranteed a high-quality product. By eliminating the middlemen and exploitive buyers, Fair Trade guarantees a price, which allows for producers to cover the costs of production and sustain their family. The additional money the producers earn translates directly to social development. They can invest the money in the future of their crops and their communities.

At the same time, Fair Trade standards ensure that buyers support small producers who are organized in democratically run cooperatives that do not allow exploitive working conditions, protect the environment, and are committed to improving the quality of life in their community. By design, this rewards small farmers who support the concepts of social justice and gives them additional resources to grow, improve, and continue their socially responsible methodologies.

According to Laura Raynolds, a sociologist from Colorado State University with the Fair Trade Research Group, "Fair Trade certification [is an] example of attempts to build alternative production and consumption networks. Fair Trade helps an increasing number of coffee drinkers align their taste for specialty coffee and values supporting social and ecological justice with enhanced options for small-scale farmer livelihoods. In this way Fair Trade certifications offer a technology to help re-embed economic relationships within social values."[6]

Linking the social and economic development of small-producer cooperatives, Fair Trade organizations hope to "improve the livelihoods and well-beings of producers by improving market access, strengthening producers' organizations, paying a better price, and providing continuity in the trading relationship."[7]

Using economic tools, FLO empowers producers and encourages social development, ensuring that human rights are upheld, the environment is protected, and economic security is made a reality.

FAIR TRADE CERTIFICATION AND LABELING

Fair Trade Certified coffee meets the basic FLO standards, and it permits more than 800,000 producers, workers, and their dependants in fifty countries to benefit from being labeled Fair Trade.

First and foremost, Fair Trade coffee is grown under conditions that support social development. The cooperatives that produce the coffee comprise small farmers and cafeicultores (coffee producers), not large plantations that rely on sweat labor. The Fair Trade Certification purports to guarantee that the farmers always receive a cost-covering price, ensuring that they can feed their families and plant from year to year. These farmers are organized in democratically structured, nondiscriminatory cooperatives that are administered transparently. The additional revenue earned from the coffee promotes social and economical development of small farmers.

These standards make certain that the cooperatives value and uphold the concepts of Fair Trade and secure the future of social development in the Fair Trade coffee community. Fair Trade Certification guarantees that the coffee communities have the ability to develop economically. Cooperatives receive a Fair Trade Premium of five U.S. cents per pound for regular coffee or fifteen U.S. cents per pound for organic coffee, and must use the additional money to support socioeconomic development. According to FLO, Fair Trade coffee also protects the rights of cafeicultores. Coffee must be produced without forced labor or involuntary prison labor. Child labor is not used, and all cafeicultores have the right to collectively bargain and form unions.

These standards signify that the coffee was produced in a manner that does not exploit the workers and that helps to improve working conditions.

Environmental development is also an important aspect of Fair Trade coffee. Often, coffee is produced under conditions that degrade the environment, endangering the health and safety of those who work the land and jeopardizing the future of production in the area. Fair Trade coffee is produced in a way that protects the natural environment and encourages long-term planning, which includes reforestation and preservation. The ultimate goal is to ensure the sustainability of the land and begin to rebuild the entire ecosystem.

Because these cooperatives meet the Fair Trade standards, the producers receive a floor price of $1.26 per pound for conventional coffee and $1.41 for organic coffee. This represents a significant increase over the open-market price or the price paid by middlemen. Fair Trade organizations are able to do this by developing direct, long-term relationships with producer cooperatives, avoiding the many levels of exploitive mediation. They are able to facilitate the work of the

EDUCATE

Read *The Conscious Consumer* by Rose Benz Ericson. Learn about the Fair Trade movement from the many informational websites on the subject. Visit a local Fair Trade store and talk to the employees about the movement. Then spread the word, encouraging your friends and family to buy Fair Trade products and asking your local grocers to consider carrying foods and other products that are Fair Trade certified.

ACTIVATE

- Buy home decor and gifts for friends and family from Fair Trade shops or online from Fair Trade organizations.

- Drink Fair Trade coffee: brew it yourself or ask for it at your favorite café.

- Buy Fair Trade candy and distribute it on Halloween (packages are available at Global Exchange's online store at *www. globalexchange.org*).

- Put in some volunteer hours at a local Fair Trade shop or volunteer to help a Fair Trade organization at the national level.

- Lobby government officials to support Fair Trade.

work of the cooperatives directly, providing pre-financing and technical support and ensuring a sustainable market for Fair Trade cooperatives over time.

Fair Trade cooperatives are revolutionary in that they allow traditionally disempowered producers to mobilize, to grow into second- and third-level cooperatives that represent thousands of producers, and to become a force politically. Where governments can ignore individual farmers with ease, cooperatives leverage the collective strength of producers and can thus create change on a broad scale.

Women's empowerment is another critical aspect of the Fair Trade movement. While agricultural goods are predominantly produced by men, crafts and textiles are overwhelmingly the realm of women. They provide women with the space to empower themselves, to develop cooperatives, and to gain experience in business even as their work preserves cultural identities through the re-creation of traditional textile designs. Fair Trade crafts open a venue for women to earn a dignified, sustainable income through which they can support themselves and their families.

Many products are labeled or certified as Fair Trade. They bear an IFAT, TransFair USA, or Fair Trade Federation seal. Any product with one of these seals has been externally verified at both the cooperative level and the business level. In the United States, Fair Trade Certified coffee, tea, rice, mangos, bananas, cocoa, pineapples, and sugar are available, as are Fair Trade crafts and locally grown produce.

BEYOND A CONSUMER MOVEMENT

Undoubtedly, Fair Trade purchases are important and make significant differences in the lives of producer communities. However, the consumer angle of Fair Trade is just one small piece of a much broader movement. At its core, Fair Trade is not about simply buying specific products; it is about empowering communities. It is about working in solidarity with producer communities, listening deeply to their experiences, and moving forward collaboratively to build an alternative economic structure based on dignity and sustainability.

UNITED STUDENTS FOR FAIR TRADE AND THE FAIR TRADE STUDENT MOVEMENT

In many ways, United Students for Fair Trade (USFT) is the progressive engine of the Fair Trade movement. The three-year-old international organization is a network of student organizations advocating Fair Trade products, policies, and principles. The core objective of USFT is to raise the awareness of and expand the demand for Fair Trade Certified products, such as coffee and crafts, both on campuses and in communities.

Since the beginnings of Fair Trade, students have put pressure on their campus food services to convert all of the campus coffee to

100 percent Fair Trade offerings. More than two hundred campuses have been successful in ether full or partial conversions, increasing demand for Fair Trade coffee by more than two million pounds. An increasing number of students are getting involved in the movement, hosting speaker tours, holding Fair Trade crafts sales, working with farm workers, launching banana campaigns, traveling to the places where producers and artisans work and live, and rocking the movement.

Students have also been at the forefront of campaigns targeting large transnational corporations like Proctor & Gamble and Kraft to source Fair Trade coffees. Working with local community groups and diverse faith communities, students have catalyzed Fair Trade coffee conversions and sparked trade justice advocacy events nationwide.

USFT and students across the country have been a constant force pushing the Fair Trade movement forward since its nascent stages. We continue to push ourselves and movement allies to evaluate our roles in recreating oppressive systems. We struggle to build an anti-oppressive movement that listens deeply and learns from the experiences of traditionally marginalized groups of people—from people of color to women to disabled individuals. We strive to redefine power dynamics between northern consumers and southern producers, attempting to build a southern-driven movement that responds to the assets and needs of producer communities, working in solidarity to redefine a global system.

"Action springs not from thought, but from a readiness for responsibility."
—DIETRICH BONHOEFFER

Another place where USFT broadens the definition of Fair Trade is within U.S. boundaries. While most Fair Trade organizations focus exclusively on ameliorating poverty, providing dignified labor and living-wage solutions in developing countries, USFT is unwilling to ignore the struggles of workers in our country. It makes no sense for us to support the struggle of Mexican farmers, but then refuse to acknowledge our responsibility in dealing with the unfair trade policies our government imposes. Students are taking a stand for Fair Trade principles both at home and abroad. We work with domestic Fair Trade initiatives, including farm-worker rights, supporting family farms and community-supported agriculture, organized labor, and sweat-free communities.

TRADE POLICY

In the global North, we have power and privilege well beyond our roles as consumers. Many of us participate in the political process, voting, campaigning, and advocating for policies that make sense. We have a responsibility to hold our government accountable to the developing world and to the millions of people worldwide who are affected by U.S. trade policy.

One significant way we have done this in the past has been through research of and opposition to free trade agreements. Policies like the North American Free Trade Agreement (NAFTA), the Central American-Dominican Republic Free Trade Agreement (CAFTA-DR), or the Free Trade Area of the Americas (FTAA) threaten lives and livelihoods in agricultural communities. Past agreements have weakened workers' rights, displaced small farmers, degraded the environment, and expedited a race to the bottom. Additionally, World Trade Organization policies like these are made in non-democratic, non-transparent, and non-representative ministerials that ignore the voices of the people who will be affected most profoundly and, instead, privilege corporations.

In addition to protesting detrimental international policies, students will play an important role in upcoming domestic legislation. According to Oxfam America, U.S. taxpayers subsidize as much as $16 billion in commodity support payments to U.S. agricultural producers. An overwhelming 78 percent of these subsidies are directed at just 8 percent of producers—large-scale farms that drive family farmers off the land and threaten rural life throughout the Midwest and elsewhere.

These misguided subsidies create the conditions for overproduction, which in turn leads to dumping U.S. commodities like cotton or corn on international markets at prices well below the cost of production. Farmers in developing countries cannot compete, driving them further into poverty.

WHAT YOU CAN DO

In the midst of this powerful global movement, there are so many ways for people to get involved. Put your passion into action!

RELATE. Perhaps the most powerful opportunity is to build face-to-face relationships with people. Get to know the activists in your community and get activated. Move outside your community and build relationships with people from different ethnic, socioeconomic, or faith communities. Move outside your borders and learn with a cooperative community. Challenge your assumptions and learn from the experiences of people who come from a radically different place.

EDUCATE. Learn about the global market and the ways that U.S.

agricultural and foreign policies affect communities around the world. Read the news and seek out alternative forms of media. Learn more about the coffee crisis, social and environmental sustainability, cooperative movements, commodity dumping, the World Trade Organization, the disappearance of family farms, and organized labor. Think about what an alternative system would look like and explore ways that your life interconnects with others in the developing world.

ACTIVATE. Get involved in your community! Make a conscious choice. Attend Fair Trade awareness and advocacy events, host a crafts sale, fill out a comment card at your grocery store, lobby your school or workplace to carry Fair Trade products, or hold a direct action. Host a Fair Trade coffee "cupping" at your local coffee shop. Buy locally grown foods and Community Supported Agriculture (CSA). Set up a table at an international music event or host a social-justice film night. The opportunities are endless.

PRAY

Lord, we were created to work even before the fall, when You set us in the Garden of Eden to work the earth. When we work, we hope that what we do yields enough to fill our needs and even make us a profit, yet there are many around the world who work their fingers raw and still go hungry, or who cannot work because there is no work to be found. We pray that those who toil away creating goods for the consumption of others would be compensated fairly and treated with dignity by their employers, receiving fair wages and working in clean, safe environments. And we pray that those who are looking for decent work will be able to find it so that they may support themselves and their loved ones and build stronger communities. For You are the giver of all good things, and to You we send up glory, to the Father, and the Son, and the Holy Spirit. Amen.

INFLUENCE. Social capital is a grossly undervalued asset. The work you do and the decisions you make directly influence the people in your network. Talk to your friends and family about Fair Trade and support their discovery processes. Spread the word at school, work, or your place of worship, and advocate those networks to buy Fair Trade products.

LOBBY. You can affect policy at a local, national, and international level. Lobby your local government to adopt a Fair Trade resolution, to exclusively brew Fair Trade coffee in municipal buildings, or to support CSA. On a national level, you can advocate for trade policies that make sense in the developing world, oppose free trade agreements that undermine democracy, and support legislation that asks the U.S. government to exclusively buy Fair Trade coffee. Make yourself heard at an international level as well. Write letters to the World Trade Organization or rally at the Ministerials.

BOYCOTT. Each purchase you make is a political statement. Think about the products you consume and consider the conditions under which they were grown or produced. Make a commitment to buy products that reflect your values. Ethically produced goods may cost more, but choosing products that empower rather than exploit makes a difference in the lives of producers and sends a message to corporations around the world that consumers will not support the dominant system of oppression.

Keep struggling! Know that the work you are doing is critical and part of a much larger struggle. "I used to think that the Fair Trade struggle was just our own ... but it fills me with joy to realize that there are other people struggling for Fair Trade around the world," said Alfredo Rayo, a student leader from Cooperativa Orgánica in La Corona, Nicaragua, as we traveled together throughout northern Nicaragua.

As our group of USFT students worked with Fair Trade coffee cooperative student leaders, I began to understand what it meant to be part of a global solidarity movement. "Today there is a new form of solidarity being built," said Pedro Haslam, the general manager of CECOCAFEN, as we stood on a balcony overlooking the coffee fields surrounding Matagalpa. "One part we do here, and the other part you do up North. The harder you work, the more communities we can reach, until one day we will change the relationships of the world so the central theme will be one of social justice."

Fair Trade is truly revolutionary; it is a movement not simply about encouraging northern consumers to purchase labeled products, but about developing cross-cultural relationships, about listening deeply, about redefining the capitalist model, about working together to empower communities, and about restoring the humanity to global trade.

JOE CURNOW is a National Organizer and Convergence coordinator for United Students for Fair Trade. Originally from Colorado, she graduated with honors from Northwestern University with degrees in policy and international studies.

MEXICO
SCALE OF MILES
0 25 50 75 100 150 200
GULF OF MEXICO
GULF OF CAMPECHE
GULF OF TEHUANTEPEC
Galveston
MATAGORDA ISL
Corpus Christi
PADRE ISL.
Piedras Negras (Porfirio Diaz)
Laredo
Nuevo Laredo
Guerrero
Mier
Rio Grande City
Brownsville
Matamoros
Reynosa
Camargo
NUEVO LEON
Cadereyta
Montemorelos
Linares
S. Fernando
L. de la Madre
Jimenez
Victoria
Tepehuaje
Ocampo
Xicotencatl
Pesca
Tampico
L. Tamiahua
Tula
Cardenas
Huejutla
Tuxpan
Molango
Zimapan
Nautla
Jicaltepec
HIDALGO
Pachuca
Jalapa
Vera Cruz
Tula
Toluca
Tlaxcala
Puebla
Cuernavaca
Atlixco
Orizaba
Cordova
Alvarado
Santiago Tuxtla
Tehuacan
Taxco
Chiautla
Tuxtepec
Juan Evangelista
Ixtlan
Etla
Oaxaca
Villa Alta
OAXACA
Chilapa
Acapulco
GUERRERO
Ometepec
Ocotlan
Juquila
Tehuantepec
Salina Cruz
Jamiltepec
Pochutla
Pt. Angel
B. del Suchiate
Huimanguillo
Montecristo
San Cristobal Las Ca
Chiapa
Comitan
Tonola
San Juan Bautista
Zamora
Morelia
Apatzin
MICHOACAN

HUNGER

BY REV. DAVID BECKMANN

"FEEDING THE HUNGRY IS A GREATER WORK
THAN RAISING THE DEAD."
—SAINT JOHN CHRYSOSTOM

Rosalba Garcia Ogarrio, a widow and mother of six, lives in the southern mountains of Oaxaca, Mexico. Her family is of Zapotec origin, like most families who live in their village and in nearby communities. "Our family struggles to make ends meet, but we are the rule, not the exception," she says. "We seldom have money to buy milk and other nutritious foods, and sometimes I have very little food to give my children. All I can give them on those occasions is a type of cinnamon tea to fill their stomachs." She knows that this lack of nutrition is the reason her children become sick often. They are vulnerable to chicken pox and other diseases.

"We don't have grandiose expectations for our future," Ogarrio says. "We simply want our government to do more to improve our lives, perhaps by creating more jobs ... I would someday like to take some steps to improve my life, including the opportunity to study and train to become a secretary."

Ogarrio and her family are not alone. More than 852 million people in the world went hungry in 2002. And in developing countries, six million children die each year, mostly from hunger-related causes.[1]

In the United States, thirty-six million people, including thirteen million children, live in households where individuals have to skip meals or eat less to make food last longer. That means one in ten U.S. households is living in hunger or is at risk of hunger.[2] Child poverty is more widespread in the United States than in any other industrialized country; at the same time, our government does less than that of any industrialized country to combat it.[3]

DONATE
Commit to making a regular monthly donation to a charity that deals with hunger.

It doesn't have to be this way. We can end hunger. The financial costs to do so are relatively slight. The United Nations Development Program estimates that the basic health and nutritional needs of the world's poorest people could be met for an additional $13 billion a year. Animal lovers in the United States and Europe spend more than that on pet food each year.

What makes the difference between millions of hungry people and a world where all are fed? Only a change in priorities. Only the will to end hunger.

Hunger exists not because the world doesn't produce enough

food—we have the experience and the technology right now to end the problem—but because it is not distributed equitably.

It would take a modest effort to end global hunger and malnutrition. Hunger is a political condition, and overcoming it will require a change in politics. Given the fact that humankind has the means to end hunger, its persistence in God's world is a scandal.

WE CAN END CHRONIC HUNGER

Some doubt that ending hunger is really possible. We've all grown up hearing about starving people in other parts of the world. Even in the United States, the world's wealthiest nation, it is not uncommon to see people on street corners asking for money, standing in a soup-kitchen lines, or going to food pantries for emergency assistance.

Christians act from faith in Jesus Christ, from the "conviction of things not seen" (Heb. 11:1, NASB). We do what we do, not because we are convinced that it will solve every problem, but because we believe it is morally the right thing to do.

Yet even the historical evidence is encouraging. Much has been achieved in the last few decades. When Bread for the World began in 1974, about one-third of people in the developing world were undernourished. Now that number has dropped to about one-sixth.

Since 1960, adult literacy in sub-Saharan Africa has increased by more than 280 percent. In East Asia, infant mortality has declined by more than 70 percent. In Latin America and the Caribbean, childhood mortality under age five has fallen by more than 75 percent. In South Asia, life expectancy has risen by 46 percent. Development assistance from the United States has played an important role in all these successes.

So while the problem of hunger is still overwhelming—scandalously large—progress has been made. And much more is possible—and necessary.

THE BIBLE CALLS US TO CARE

God feeds us with the Bread of Life and with daily bread, and it is our job to share these gifts with others. *Grace* means "gift"—first and foremost, the gift of God's undeserved love for us in Jesus Christ, whose life, death, and resurrection rescued us from sin and gave us eternal life. In Jesus, God reaches out in love to all people—to those who don't have enough to eat and to those who find it easy to ignore others in need. Because we are saved by grace for the purpose of giving our lives to works of love (Eph. 2:8-10), God's grace can powerfully motivate us to help end hunger.

There are dozens of verses in the Bible that call Christians to feed the hungry and care for the poor, clearly indicating that these two mandates are central to being followers of Jesus. The prophet Isaiah says, "Is not this the kind of fasting I have chosen: to loose the chains of injustice and untie the cords of the yoke, to set the oppressed free and break every yoke? Is it not to share your food with the hungry and to provide the poor wanderer with shelter?" (Isa. 58:6-7, TNIV). The book of Matthew says that each time we feed the hungry, give water to the thirsty, welcome the stranger, clothe the naked, care for the sick, and visit the prisoner, we are doing it for Jesus Himself (Matt. 25:40).

Interestingly, the verse most often cited when American Christians talk about overcoming hunger and poverty is Jesus' statement, "For you always have the poor with you; but you do not always have Me" (Matt. 26:11; John 12:8, NASB). A popular interpretation is this: "Jesus said we'll always have the poor with us. That is just a reality. So there is really no point in trying to overcome poverty or extreme hunger."

That explanation, however, takes the verse out of context. Here's another way to understand those words: "You will always have the poor with you, so you should make working with the poor a way of life." Reading the verse that way strips away any excuse for apathy. It becomes a statement about Christian identity rather than about poverty as an eternal reality.

THE CASE FOR ADVOCACY

In Scripture, God calls us to open our hearts and hands to people in need and reminds us that the way we treat vulnerable people translates directly to the way we treat Him. "Those who oppress the poor insult their Maker, but those who help the poor honor him" (Prov. 14:31, NLT). His call to care for the poor extends to those in power. Through Isaiah, God issues a warning to "those who make unjust laws, to those who issue oppressive decrees, to deprive the poor of their rights and withhold justice from the oppressed of my people" (Isa. 10:1-2, TNIV). God calls on each of us to speak up for those who are hungry and oppressed, just as Moses spoke to the powers of his day. Jesus and His disciples, too, challenged both religious and political authorities to do what was right.

Why should Christians engage in advocacy? Why do we need to get the government involved? Can't we just deal with the problem of hunger through charity and faith-based efforts? The starting point for advocacy is faith. Our faith teaches us that God cares about the world and wants all people to share in the abundant resources of creation. When so many people are unable to partake of that abundance, we need to take action and make a change.

Churches and charities cannot address poverty on a systemic level. People are hungry because they are poor. To help hungry people, therefore, we need to address both their immediate needs and the larger picture.

For example, if a farmer in Africa can produce enough grain to feed his family and have some left over to sell, but does not have access to a road to get to the market, then he will remain poor. Governments are responsible for building infrastructures like roads and regulating trade rules and working conditions.

> "Love and business and family and religion and art and patriotism are nothing but shadows of words when a man's starving."
> —O. HENRY

Becoming involved in advocacy helps us move from a charity model of assistance to a model that seeks justice for hungry people. Charity is good and necessary during times of crisis, but ultimately only addresses the symptoms of hunger, not the causes. Over the long term it creates a dependent population subject to the goodwill and generosity of others. Justice creates a society where people are able to provide for themselves and their families by earning a wage. God requires both charity and justice, and justice can often be achieved through the mechanism of government.

In this country, we have the gift of citizenship and the responsibility to use its power to promote public justice and address the root causes of hunger. Since our faith calls us to seek justice, we voice our concerns to those who have the power to implement justice on a large scale. raising our voices to tell government leaders, "We are concerned about the things that matter to God, and we will hold you accountable for those things." Government is not the only mechanism to deal with hunger, but it is an institution that has a significant role to play in providing for the welfare of its people.

Mary Helene Mele, a Bread for the World member from Arlington, Virginia, recalls her first lobbying effort in 1987. Right before a jog, she was reading her Bread for the World newsletter and heard, for the first time, about the Special Supplemental Nutrition Program for Women, Infants, and Children (WIC). WIC provides additional food, nutrition education, and medical screening to low-income pregnant women, new mothers, infants, and children up to age five. In the newsletter she read about the importance of getting increased funding for this program and how a study had shown that WIC saved money in public health costs down the road.

While jogging, she stopped at the local public library and saw a sign advertising that her representative was at the post office to meet constituents. She jogged to the post office with no intention of speaking to him, since she had never met him before and was sweaty and wearing running shorts. When she arrived, however, there was no crowd—it was just her and her congressman. She almost left without saying a word, and then reminded herself, "I need to go talk to him about the hungry women and children." She asked him to support an increase in funding for WIC.

The next week she called his office to follow up. He had committed to supporting the WIC funding increase.

"I forget the numbers now, but at the time I figured out that if I fed the homeless every night of the week for the rest of my life, I might not have given as much as I did that ten minutes in the post office," Mele says.

ADVOCACY HAS AN IMPACT

By and large, Christians understand that we are called to care for those who are hungry. Most churchgoers have given donations for a food drive or volunteered at a local food pantry or soup kitchen. Far fewer have advocated to the federal and state government on behalf of the poor and hungry, asking that public policies reflect our moral obligation to care for the most vulnerable among us. Some people may feel isolated from the sometimes-confusing legislative process. Others do not really believe their voice will have an impact on their elected representatives. You should know: legislators really are listening.

Several years ago, during a legislative campaign, a member of our government-relations department at Bread for the World received a call from a congressional aide, who said, "Tell me more about this legislation. We've gotten lots of letters about it." The staff member gladly did so, explaining how the legislation would benefit hungry people. At the end of the conversation she asked how many letters the aide had received. The aide replied, "Quite a few." She pushed, "Well, how many is quite a few?" The answer? Eight.

Eight letters. That is all it took for an elected official to ask his aide to call and find out more about the legislation and ultimately to vote to support it.

In 1999, four advocates from Alabama made a huge difference with their congressman, Rep. Spencer Bachus. He was chair of the international committee of the House Banking Committee, where all congressional action on debt relief must start. Bread for the World members Pat Pelham and Elaine VanCleave and two friends from Independent Presbyterian Church flew from Birmingham, Alabama, to Washington, D.C., to meet with him. Speaking from

74

their Christian faith, they educated Rep. Bachus on the effect of unpayable debt on people in developing countries. "I don't know much about economics or international finance," VanCleave explained. "But I do know that about thirty thousand children die every day from hunger and other preventable causes, and, as a mother, that really bothers me ... it would help a lot if you would sponsor this Jubilee legislation."

Rep. Bachus, a Southern Baptist, is a straightforward Christian. When the Banking Committee held its hearing on poor-country debt, Bachus said, "If we don't write off some of this debt, poor people in these countries will be suffering for the rest of their lives. And we'll be suffering a lot longer than that." Ultimately, he became an outspoken and influential advocate for debt relief, which led to the eventual passage of the legislation.

EDUCATE
Read *Rich Christians in an Age of Hunger* by Ronald Sider and other resources about the hunger problem, and then spread the word to those in your community.

HUNGER IN THE UNITED STATES

Who, exactly, suffers from hunger?

Abra is a thirty-eight-year-old single mother who lives with her son David, eight, in Virginia. She has a college degree and once had a moderately well-paying job in the health care industry. However, increasingly severe health problems have forced her to take part-time jobs. She has a hard time keeping these because she misses work frequently for doctor's appointments. Her elderly parents live off Social Security and are unable to help her financially, although they do watch David while she is at work. At one point, she and David had to move temporarily into a homeless shelter. Now living on her own again, she is not always able to provide healthy meals for David and herself. Because they frequently eat off the value menus at fast-food restaurants, they are both overweight, which only adds to Abra's health problems. When David is in school, he receives free breakfast and lunch. But in the summer, Abra sometimes skips meals so that David will have enough to eat. She always volunteers to help cook and clean up after meals at church so she can bring the extra food home.

Dorothy is a seventy-eight-year-old widow in Tampa, Florida. She lives off $550 per month in Social Security benefits that must cover rent, utilities, transportation, and medications. She spends part of her income providing food for her great-granddaughter, whom she cares for while her granddaughter works. To make ends meet, Dorothy volunteers at a food cooperative, where she is able to buy bulk food at wholesale prices in exchange for her volunteer labor. Without this program, she and her great-grandchild would sometimes go hungry.

Although many think that *hungry* people and *homeless* people are the same, the problem of hunger reaches far beyond homelessness. While the thought of thirty-six million people at risk of hunger may be surprising, it is the faces of those thirty-six million individuals that would probably shock you most.

The face of hunger is the older couple who have worked hard for their entire lives, only to find their savings wiped out by unavoidable medical bills. It is a single mother who has to choose whether the salary from her minimum-wage job will go to buy food or pay rent. It is a child who struggles to concentrate on his schoolwork because his family couldn't afford dinner the night before. In fact, a December 2004 survey by the U.S. Conference of Mayors estimated that 56 percent of those requesting emergency food assistance were either young children or their parents.[4]

Children are twice as likely than adults to live in a household where someone experiences hunger and food insecurity. One in ten adults live in such circumstances, compared to one in five children.[5]

A study commissioned in 2001 by America's Second Harvest, the nation's largest network of food banks, found that almost 40 percent of households seeking assistance from emergency food banks had one or more family member currently employed.[6] Hunger is becoming a growing problem among the working poor.

There are various reasons many working Americans are unable to feed their families. From a broader economic perspective, we can point to the fact

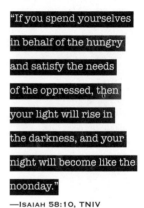

"If you spend yourselves in behalf of the hungry and satisfy the needs of the oppressed, then your light will rise in the darkness, and your night will become like the noonday."
—Isaiah 58:10, TNIV

that the United States has the highest wage inequality of any industrialized nation.[7] People can work full-time, low-skill jobs and still not make enough money to maintain a basic standard of living—buying food, paying rent and medical bills, buying clothes for children, and affording a car to travel to work.

Simply supplying food seldom gets to the roots of hunger. In the United States, food pantries provide urgently needed help. But food assistance is less important to overcoming hunger than job opportunities. Empowering people—providing them with opportunities or helping them cultivate an awareness of what they can do to improve their lives—is one of the most important ways to beat hunger and poverty.

INTERNATIONAL HUNGER

"There is no way to get used to hunger," says Adilesi Faisoni, who lives in the African country of Malawi, where finding enough to eat can be a daily struggle for many people.[8] "All the time something is moving in your stomach. You feel the emptiness. You feel your intestines moving. They are too empty, and they are searching for something to fill up on."

At its most extreme, hunger claims lives. Faisoni lost both her husband and her daughter to hunger in 2003. They died within a month of each other, unable to subsist on pumpkin leaves and wild vegetables—the family's only nourishment during the months of December through March, when Malawi suffers an annual food shortage.

Only a small percentage of hunger deaths are caused by starvation. Most hunger-related deaths are the result of chronic undernutrition, which weakens the body's ability to ward off diseases prevalent in poverty-stricken communities. Most hungry people have some food, but not enough food or not enough of the right kinds of food.

Famines, which most people believe are caused by natural disasters, are just the tip of the iceberg, responsible for about 3 percent of the approximately seven million hunger-

ACTIVATE

• Instead of giving money to the corner panhandler who says he's hungry, take him out to dinner.

• Make small care packages with healthy snacks and gift certificates to fast-food restaurants and pass them out when asked for money.

• Volunteer at your local soup kitchen regularly.

• Lobby your local and state representatives to propose and support legislation that provides for a higher level of aid to the hungry around the world.

related deaths that occur in a typical year.[9]

Currently 852 million people, mainly in developing countries, are chronically or acutely undernourished. Although progress against hunger has been made in East Asia, the majority of those who are malnourished live in China (114 million) and India (221 million). But sub-Saharan Africa, with 204 million people hungry, is the only region in the world where the statistic is increasing.[10]

When people actually starve to death—where virtually no food is available—the cause is primarily political, not weather-related. In North Korea, countless people have starved because of the government's unwillingness to give up on failed economic policies. In Sudan, millions are threatened with starvation because of an ongoing military conflict that has devastated the country's ability to produce food—and because the government restricts the flow of emergency relief.

At the same time, India—a country that experiences chronic hunger—has eliminated the threat of famine and mass starvation. Nobel prizewinning economist Amartya Sen explains that "open journalism and adversarial politics" have made it impossible for local governments "to get away with neglecting prompt and extensive anti-famine measures at the first sign of a famine." India's free press and the investigative role played by journalists as well as opposition party members require politicians to prevent and respond to frequent dips in food supply and occasional droughts.

WHAT YOU CAN DO

To be an effective anti-hunger advocate, an important step is to educate yourself about the realities of hunger and our public policies. Nearly half of U.S. voters believe that either welfare or foreign aid is the biggest item in the federal budget. In fact, nutrition programs and welfare together amount to only 3 percent of federal spending. Foreign aid takes up less than 1 percent of the budget, and only a small portion of that is focused on sustainable development and humanitarian assistance.

It is also important to take note when policies change in a positive way. As mentioned earlier, in recent years anti-hunger advocates have won significant victories that benefit those who battle hunger. In 2003 President Bush proposed, and Congress established, the Millennium Challenge Account as a new international assistance initiative focused on poverty reduction, making the largest funding increase in decades to combat hunger, poverty, and disease in the developing world. Faithful advocacy helped persuade Congress to approve a $2 billion increase in poverty-focused development assistance—up 33 percent from the previous year!

Another powerful change has been the continued campaign to forgive crushing debt in developing nations. During 1999 and 2000, at the peak of the worldwide Jubilee 2000 grassroots campaign, Congress freed up more than $2.5 billion, including $545 million toward the U.S. contribution to the debt-relief plan. The World Bank and other international financial institutions also announced a major shift in policy that would tie debt-relief efforts to poverty reduction. That shift has made a difference, leading to dramatic expansions of school enrollment in some African countries. Many more children, especially girls, are now learning to read and write. That campaign truly captured a God-given moment. Who would have thought that debt relief could motivate so many people of faith into action?

But positive changes are not automatic. Advocacy also requires recognizing places where work still needs to be done to bring about justice for people who need food. The Federal Nutrition Programs (food stamps, WIC, the School Breakfast and Lunch Programs) are often popular targets for funding cuts among legislators trying to balance the budget, despite the fact that they are the fastest and most direct way of addressing the needs of hungry people in this country. Raising the minimum wage is necessary if low-income workers are ever going to be able to support their families. The federal budget must not be balanced on the backs of the needy.

Internationally, U.S. leaders have made many pledges of increased poverty-focused development assistance. We have already seen significant growth, but advocates must ensure that those promises are fully kept. Continued debt relief and reform of trade rules to allow fair trade for everyone in global markets are just as important as increasing aid.

Finally, to be an advocate, you must get involved. Writing a letter and visiting your Congressional representatives are still the most effective ways to make your voice heard. And joining with others to do that work magnifies your impact.

The Global Call to Action Against Poverty has launched campaigns in more than eighty countries. Supporters wear white bands to indicate their commitment to ending extreme poverty and

PRAY

Lord, as You once filled the Israelites with manna, please fill all those who, for whatever reason, are unable to fill themselves with healthy foods. And grant us strength as we go about helping our hungry neighbors, offering them both food to fill their empty stomachs and love to fill their hungering hearts. Amen.

hunger. The U.S. version is called the ONE Campaign. More than two million members have signed the ONE Declaration, calling on our government to make ending poverty and hunger a priority by increasing development assistance by 1 percent of the national budget.

Take a first step for hunger advocacy. Then another. Then another. Educate yourself and make your voice heard. Sign up for the ONE Campaign at *www.bread.org/onestep*. Join Bread for the World. Become part of your church's or denomination's hunger program or some other local campaign.

Jesus told the story of a persistent widow. She went to court again and again to ask for justice, and the judge ultimately granted her request. Jesus tells us, "And will not God bring about justice for his chosen ones, who cry out to him day and night? Will he keep putting them off? I tell you, he will see that they get justice, and quickly" (Luke 18:7-8, TNIV). Hungry people are asking for this justice, too, and they must not be denied.

DAVID BECKMANN is a Lutheran pastor and was commissioned at his ordination to be a missionary economist. He served in Bangladesh for a church-related relief and development agency, then worked at the World Bank for fifteen years. He has served as president of Bread for the World and Bread for the World Institute since 1991. He lives in Alexandria, Virginia, with his wife; they have two sons.

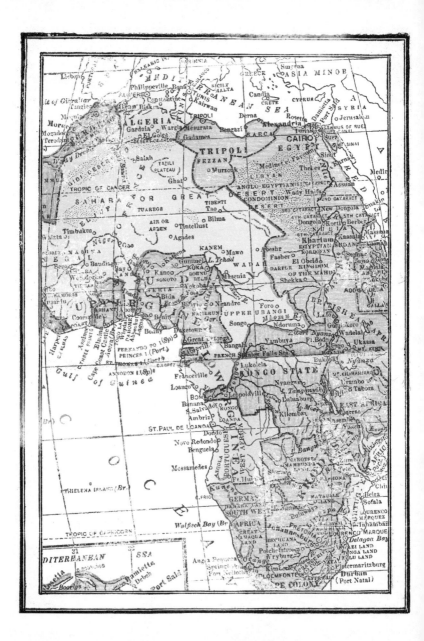

CHAPTER SIX

HIV/AIDS

BY JENA LEE

"THIS IS OUR MOMENT, THIS IS OUR TIME, THIS IS OUR CHANCE TO STAND UP FOR WHAT IS RIGHT. THREE THOUSAND AFRICANS, MOSTLY CHILDREN, DIE EVERY DAY OF MOSQUITO BITES. WE CAN FIX THAT. NINE THOUSAND PEOPLE DYING EVERY DAY DIE OF A PREVENTABLE, TREATABLE DISEASE LIKE AIDS. WE HAVE GOT THE DRUGS. WE CAN HELP THEM." —BONO

Saturday is my favorite day of the week. It's a day without alarm clocks, long meetings, and pressing deadlines. As a child, Saturdays were for cartoons, pajamas, and Lucky Charms, for softball games, sleepovers, and birthday parties. They meant a break from the grind of homework and studying for tests. Even now, my roommates and I have a Saturday-morning ritual where we stay in our pajamas as long as we can, indulging in maple syrup-soaked waffles and enjoying the day that embodies freedom and relaxation after an exhausting week of work.

But my fondness for Saturdays changed when I went to Africa.

Violet Asya is seventeen years old. She lives in Kenya, and for her, Saturdays are the saddest days of the year. As in many parts of Africa, funerals in western Kenya take place on Saturdays. Violet buried her mother on a Saturday in 2003 and her father on a Saturday in 2004. She is under the care of her ailing grandmother and often does not have enough money to feed herself or her brothers and sisters. Two months ago, she dropped out of school because no one can pay for her school fees. In the last year, she has attended five burials for some of her closest friends. Violet lives in a village where, on average, five people die each week from HIV/AIDS. The pandemic in Africa continues to take millions of lives and has taken Saturday hostage for its keeping. While Violet enjoys spending her free time playing soccer and reading books, her Saturdays are typically spent at a funeral for yet another loved one who has been lost to the HIV/AIDS crisis.

DONATE
Make a donation to
an AIDS organization.

WHY IS THIS A PRESSING ISSUE IN THE WORLD?

Violet Asya's story is a hint of how millions have been affected by AIDS. Because of its growing devastation, the global HIV/AIDS pandemic has been termed the greatest humanitarian crisis in the world today. More than twenty million people have died from AIDS in the last twenty years. Twenty-five million people live with HIV in Africa as the disease spreads rapidly across different parts of the world. According to the Joint United Nations Programme on HIV/AIDS (UNAIDS), in India, 5.1 million people are HIV-positive—the largest number of people living with HIV outside of South Africa.[1] It's growing in Asia, home to 60 percent of the world's population. It's spreading in Russia. While difficult to accept, it's growing in our own country as well.

We live in an increasingly shrinking world. The whole world fits in little electronic boxes. We have twenty-four/seven news coverage, Internet at our fingertips, input constantly screaming for our attention. But this calls for us to be aware of our neighbors, to reach outward and engage with them. The overwhelming tragedy of AIDS in our world may cause some to shake their heads with a sense of helplessness. But I have met Violet, and I have seen hope. My hope is that the closeness of AIDS to our lives will inspire you to help alleviate the suffering and the injustice that cascade from the scourge of the disease.

AIDS ON A BODY, ON A CONTINENT

James Luthuli is a passionate and smart young man in central Kenya who is HIV-positive. The Human Immunodeficiency Virus is transmitted through sex, blood transfusions and other bodily fluids, or childbirth. HIV progressively weakens the immune system and reduces a person's ability to fight basic diseases, leading eventually to Acquired Immune Deficiency Syndrome (AIDS).

James tells me that he has experienced a wide range of symptoms from HIV. Sometimes his skin gets open sores that hurt simply from exposure to the air. He often suffers from high fevers and a loss of appetite, which combine to produce severe weight loss. James is prone to a wide spectrum of illnesses, many of which are not life-threatening for healthy individuals. He told me how HIV makes it hard to stay healthy. "My body is like an open house, so all these diseases can visit and attack me freely," he explained.

A few years ago, I saw an extremely sick two-year-old boy. He was lying rather sadly in the ICU of a South African hospital. I played peekaboo with him, hiding my head behind my hands and then raising my face with a wide-eyed, big-smiled expression. I wanted to make him laugh or smile, but realized there was nothing that was going to ease the seriousness on his face. He fought for every breath as his lungs inflated and deflated rapidly, a small oxygen nasal cannula lodged in his swollen nostrils as he stared at me with discomfort and affliction.

I asked the nurse what was wrong with the boy and when he was expected to recover.

"His mother died last week from AIDS," she said. "He's HIV-positive. He has only a few more days to live." I stood in that hospital room, instantly broken. In the next moment, looking at him, tears flooded my eyes, and I felt angry. In that moment, the gut-wrenching reality of injustice filled my soul. I saw AIDS as a great enemy that took the lives of innocent children. Now when I hear the statistic that twenty million people have died of AIDS, I see that little boy, and I know that one death is too many, and that twenty million deaths is utterly, totally, conclusively, irrefutably unacceptable. Not just in my mind. For all of us.

Just as the virus attacks the weakest parts of the body, it also attacks the weakest parts of society. AIDS knows no borders and hits the poorest of us the hardest. It is a health crisis that affects the social, economic, political, spiritual, and emotional health of communities, continents, and the world. Those who are already afflicted by dire poverty are now experiencing AIDS in a way that powerfully adds lingering death to centuries of agony. The disease runs rampant among the poor, the marginalized, and the oppressed; and it takes particular care to victimize women and children.

Most African women I met were widows caring for children that were not their own. After slaying millions of Africans, HIV/AIDS has left more than fourteen million orphans. Violet's ailing grandmother, a widow, struggles every day to provide the basic needs for orphaned children of her devastated family. Her son, Violet's father, was a schoolteacher, and his wife, Violet's mother, once sold fruits and vegetables in the village. They earned enough to barely pay for Violet's food, clothing, and school fees. She and her siblings have now been at the mercy of other neighbors who are struggling just as desperately to survive because they too are caring for orphans. This, in turn, is producing a new generation with little or no means for survival.

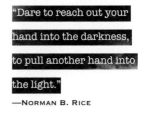

"Dare to reach out your hand into the darkness, to pull another hand into the light."
—NORMAN B. RICE

The invasion of AIDS on the developing world has imitated in real life the cinematic horrors of science fiction. It has slain adults and killed children. It has crippled the workforce, decreased life expectancy by two decades, reduced economic growth, weakened governance, disrupted marginal infrastructures, halted productivity, undermined national security, dissolved families, invited armed conflict, and impeded the health and educational development that are necessary to help impoverished communities rise above extreme poverty.

WHY SHOULD WE BE CONCERNED
ABOUT HIV/AIDS?

Americans who were not overseas in World War II, who were not in Lower Manhattan on September 11, or not in the Gulf Coast when Katrina struck struggle to grasp the impact of the HIV/AIDS pandemic. It's hard to imagine what it would be like to lose so many people in your community, to lose 8,500 people a day, every day; to have discomfort and death lurking in your path for all the days of your life; to witness the gradual collapse of your nation because people have died and many of the living are too sick to work.

Recently I met with a large multinational corporation that is dedicated to fighting the HIV/AIDS crisis in Africa through its corporate foundation. The director of the foundation said it had been difficult to understand the emergency of AIDS until he visited his employees in South Africa to learn what they'd like from the company.

"They told me they desperately needed a hearse," he said. "That's when it hit me. People in our company were losing family members by the hundreds. They needed funeral supplies. I knew AIDS was a serious deal and that we were responsible for responding to it."

In college, I spent much of my time studying historical social justice issues, with a focus on the civil rights movement and global holocausts. I remember being shocked because the world had mutely allowed injustice to triumph. There had been very little opposition. I looked back at those times of suffering and injustice and wondered, *Were there no people to speak for those without a voice? Why didn't we pressure our government to act?* I learned that while Africans, Asians, and Europeans were being slaughtered in the war that would eventually take 165 million lives, six million American mothers, many of them wearing minks and veiled hats and claiming Christian reasoning, protested the provision of aid to the victims, blaming the Jews and Europeans for their own problems.

Documentaries of the Holocaust, the Rwandan genocide, and American racial segregation have made me shake my head and say, "Never again. Not here. Not ever." Now I wonder if future documentaries will report how AIDS ripped through our world and how most of the wealthiest and best educated failed to act.

No region of the world has been spared. The projection for the spread of the pandemic is staggering. UNAIDS has named AIDS as "an extraordinary kind of crisis; it is both an emergency and a long-term development issue." The problem of AIDS is not going to go away of its own accord. Instead, it will become much worse. Many developing countries lack the resources to support, much less help, their struggling communities. Poverty has hindered the ability to rise above this crisis.

History has taught us that sickness and death in one corner of the planet will eventually affect others. But HIV/AIDS is on every continent. Why, then, are we not responding to this pandemic that is attacking our world?

WHAT ARE THE BARRIERS THAT PREVENT US FROM SERVING THOSE IN NEED?

Earlier this year, I spent a weekend taking classes on community development, sanitation, and hygiene in the developing world. People from all over the country and all walks of life had convened for these courses. During lunch breaks, I shared time with a wonderful woman whose spirit lit up our room; her enthusiasm was contagious. Sincerely concerned about the HIV/AIDS crisis, we were able to discuss how the pandemic was impacting Africa and India. We explored how to address the issue. While discussing the spread of AIDS, she stopped me in mid-sentence.

"Jena, don't you think that if they just learned to abstain, we could fix the problem?" She asked why so many people were making immoral decisions and suggested that immorality is the reason that AIDS is devastating populations in India and Africa.

I've heard this before—that if we taught others about morality, the AIDS crisis would go away. This is one of the great barriers to addressing the HIV/AIDS crisis. Paradoxically, this judgment is particularly strong in the American Christian community.

My dear friend's question sparked pain in my heart. The question offered a simple answer for a complex question. In the midst of the unjust and horrific HIV/AIDS crisis, a simple answer can beguile us. It can seem to ease affliction, guilt, and paralysis. I wish there were an easy answer, for I love to face a problem and try to fix it. Immediately. AIDS has been the hardest because its magnitude is stunning. Those who fight it have discovered that when you begin considering options, solutions become more complex. This is a very difficult foe.

Pamela Kumbuka smiles as she greets me. She is a painfully thin and quiet mother of four children, all under the age of twelve. She has a pleasant demeanor, a kind expression on a handsome face, and a powerful commitment to her young. When her husband died from malaria last year and their tiny income plummeted, their small plot of land was taken from her. She and her children have since moved in with her sister and brother-in-law, but have no source of income to support the children. Pamela spent her childhood doing the necessary tasks for daily survival. She gathered wood, walked long and difficult miles every day to carry buckets of disease-bearing water, cooked, cleaned, and helped care for her younger siblings. Unable to attend school as a child, now, as a widow, she struggles to find the means to obtain food for her children.

Her children have gone days without food, and Pamela fights against despair. I have met with women who, like Pamela, struggle to keep their children alive. Sometimes, despite the protests that come from their souls, the only way they can save the lives of their children is to sleep with men who will give them food in return.

Suppose that the man from whom Pamela receives food is HIV-positive. Now she, and every woman whose time he purchases, has an excellent chance of contracting the fatal virus. And then, through the course of living in tight quarters, it spreads. No one knows until it's too late.

What was the moral choice for Pamela? Stay sexually pure or watch her children starve to death? There is no easy answer to this complex challenge. In many cases around the world, women do not have the luxury to make the moral decisions that we have defined in the United States. Poverty and injustice have left them with different choices.

EDUCATE
Learn about the facts surrounding the HIV/AIDS pandemic and work hard to make sure those around you know the truth about the illness and how they can help those afflicted with AIDS around the world. Encourage your loved ones to set aside any biases they may have about AIDS and work to fight the disease sensitively, lovingly, and selflessly.

We might ask ourselves why it's tough to bring an AIDS conversation into the American Church. Although homosexuality accounts for only 5 to 10 percent of worldwide HIV cases, the issue of sexual activity has caused the Church to hesitate on addressing the HIV/AIDS crisis.[2] Instead of inspiring opportunities for love and engagement, the stigma of sexual immorality invites the dangerous potential for judgment and isolation of the victims. Whether from fear or ignorance, the Church has been slow to address the issue of AIDS. U2's frontman, Bono, has called the American Church the "Sleeping Giant" in reference to its response, and its inaction, to the HIV/AIDS pandemic.

The ninth chapter of John addresses injustice, brokenness, and confusion in relating a question a disciple asked Jesus: Whose fault was it that a man was born blind? Was it his fault or his parents'? Along these same lines, we could ask, "Jesus, why was this little boy born with AIDS? Whose fault was it?"

Jesus told His disciples, "It was not anyone's fault. This man was born blind"—and perhaps this baby was born HIV-positive—"so that God's mercy could be demonstrated." Then Jesus gave the blind man sight. He healed the sick, showed mercy to His children, and gave hope to the bystanders.

"Greater love has no one than this: to lay down one's life for one's friends."
—JOHN 15:13, TNIV

Ultimately, sin is to blame for HIV/AIDS. But in the scheme of the kingdom, does it matter who can be blamed and whom we might choose to judge? Is there any benefit to knowing where to point the finger in the process of reaching into the suffering with compassion and a helping hand? Blaming others to feel better about not helping is a common human habit. Even if HIV/AIDS could somehow be attributed to sexual promiscuity, is it not an equal sin to go against God's command to heal the sick and to care for the widow and the orphan (James 1:27)? Is this not the moment to see ourselves as instruments of God's work in the world?

WHAT YOU CAN DO

I am sitting in a coffee shop. But if I lift my fingers from the keyboard and close my eyes, I am again in a South African hospital ward with a beautiful dying child. I am seated in a mud-floored Kenyan hut with a hungry family, hearing them sing to God. I am standing on a narrow, dusty road to a brilliant, crimson African sunrise. The faces of the orphan, the widow, the AIDS victim, the broken, the lonely, and the hungry move their lips. If I turn off my iPod, even here in America, I can hear their labored breathing, their call for human dignity, for hope, for a chance to live and to fulfill that which God created them to be.

What do I have to offer as my body is deteriorating? How am I to expect anything better in my life if I live in a shack buried in trash? Who will love me, now that my mother has died of AIDS and I am HIV-positive? We are the downtrodden.

I hear Violet, James, and Pamela's calls as screams inside my heart. *Help*, they say, *we struggle for self-respect. We struggle against the internal killers of shame, lowliness, disability, doubt. We are poor. If you can, help me, sister.*

Sometimes we can't save the sick, but we can support them in dignity and love. We can hold the orphan. We can teach a girl to read so she can gain confidence in a frightening future. We can advocate for them. We can serve and love them. We can embrace them in prayer.

God promises that there is no such thing as a helpless situation. His redemption rises in the midst of crisis and turbulence. We are each called to do something great. Yet I fear that so many of us see the overwhelming gloom of a situation and doubt God's ability to come through the brokenness. I remind myself to not forget what happened at the cross.

ACTIVATE

• Contact an AIDS ministry and offer your services.

• Get involved with a local hospice or hospital that has a need for volunteers to minister to those with AIDS and HIV.

• Take a short-term mission trip to a country where HIV/ AIDS is rampant and offer aid to the sick and their families.

• If you have the means, consider adopting or becoming a foster parent to an infant or child with HIV/ AIDS.

• Lobby government officials to make HIV/AIDS prevention a priority.

PRAY. Isaiah 58:9 says, "Then you will call, and the Lord will answer; you will cry for help, and he will say: Here am I" (NIV).

Your prayers are necessary. God listens to the cries of the oppressed and to those who advocate for them on His behalf. In praying for our brothers and sisters across the globe, change can occur—both within the lives of those for whom you pray and within your own heart and your own life. Your prayers are powerful. I let God stir me as I pray for people who are infected and affected by AIDS. I let Him guide me where He desires, and I have never been so fulfilled in a sense of purpose or felt so aligned with Him.

GIVE. You can help Violet, James, and other brothers and sisters with financial support. I work for Blood:Water Mission and with Africare and African Leadership. These and other organizations focus on holistic, fellowship-driven, and sustainable community development to strategically assist communities most affected by AIDS.

PARTICIPATE. Our government has an abundance of resources that are needed desperately in places like Africa. In a democracy, it's our job to make the phone calls and write the letters to senators and representatives. It's their job to listen to our expectations that they immediately and substantially support AIDS programs across the globe, like the Global Fund and the President's Emergency Plan for AIDS Relief (PEPFAR).

If you want to learn more about whom to call and what to say, check out DATA (Debt, AIDS, Trade in Africa) and The ONE Campaign. Your voice is invaluable in the fight against AIDS.

LEAD. Leadership is inspiring others to become their best. If you are a student and have an interest in starting a chapter on your high-school or college campus to advocate for fighting the global AIDS pandemic, there are groups that can assist you in doing so. Acting on AIDS and Student Global AIDS Campaign are an excellent start.

It is important to remember that the AIDS crisis is happening in our own backyard. You can look up your local AIDS organization and find volunteer opportunities to help them out.

Stay informed and start conversations about the HIV/AIDS pandemic. As noted, the AIDS crisis is complex. It raises intertwined questions about justice, community development, faith, and brotherhood. Bring the conversation to the dinner table, to the small group, to the office, and into your American life.

Maintain hope and extend grace and love. There are incredible individuals across the globe, including in our own country, who are offering this hope and love to people living with AIDS. In Africa, I have met leaders of character, convictions of steel, and the determination to make a difference in someone's life.

Julie Hornby, a nurse at the Hillcrest AIDS Centre in Durban,

South Africa, once told me, "We're not curing people, but if ... you can give pride and dignity to make them part of the community, all of this is worth it." Her spirit was a Times Square neon sign that beamed, "HOPE." The world needs more Julies to seek beauty and dignity in places of sorrow and loss, to walk alongside our brothers and sisters like Violet, James, and Pamela.

I have seen firsthand that the deepest and most universal desire of people everywhere is to be loved, regardless of social, economic, racial, or physical conditions, to be treated as if Jesus were washing our dirty feet.

WHY WE CAN'T WAIT

Courageous activist Dr. Martin Luther King Jr. explained the events and forces behind the civil rights movement in his book *Why We Can't Wait*. He described the urgency for action against injustice by saying, "Perhaps it is easy for those who never felt the stinging darts of segregation to say, 'Wait.' But when you have seen vicious mobs lynch your mothers and fathers at will and drown your sisters and brothers at whim ... then you will understand why we find it difficult to wait. There comes a time when the cup of endurance runs over, and men are no longer willing to be plunged into the abyss of despair."

In the same vein, when you genuinely accept that a young girl must bury her parents while a two-year-old dies without ever stepping foot outside the hospital in which he was born, and when you understand a single mother's burning sadness in sacrificing her body to feed her children, it's simply impossible to return to the notion that nothing can be done and that the you're better off waiting for someone else to act.

In recent years, awareness of the HIV/ AIDS crisis has increased. World leaders, rock stars, actors, and other pop icons have begun to speak more urgently about the pandemic.

The problem is, that is not enough. It's not enough because AIDS still kills 8,500 people every day. It's not enough because we who have much are equipped to do more than shake our heads and say, "That's too bad."

Today is Saturday, and I'm at my desk in my home in the South. A mix of my favorite songs on iTunes is playing. A tropical storm blew out my bedroom window, and it was being repaired as Hurricane Katrina moved into three southern states, reminding us of our need to do what is right before it's too late. Bright, morning sunlight beams through the new window, and I can see shades of African crimson and remember how I was welcomed and touched by people who have less than little.

Saturday used to be my favorite day until Violet shared her life with an American nonprofit worker who asked why she didn't like Saturdays. I'm privileged to share my prayers with her

PRAY

Lord, You admonished Your disciples to "heal the sick, raise the dead, cleanse those who have leprosy, drive out demons" (Matt. 10:8, TNIV). Help us to be a rock of support to those who are afflicted with illnesses like HIV and AIDS, nurturing them with love and support until their dying day. And grant us the foresight, the wisdom, and the tools to prevent AIDS from infecting more victims. You have given to us, Your children, so freely; help us to freely give. Amen.

and to carry a tiny part of her burden through my love of Christ, my obedience to kingdom-building, and my very intentional support and advocacy of my African brothers and sisters.

Saturday is again becoming my favorite day of the week. Wherever I am, and whatever load I carry, I know I'm not alone, for I share that day with those who need sharing most.

JENA LEE is the executive director of Blood:Water Mission, a nonprofit organization founded by Jars of Clay to tangibly reduce the impact of the HIV/AIDS pandemic; to promote clean blood and clean water in Africa; and to build equitable, sustainable, and personal community links. She graduated from Whitworth College in 2004 with a political studies degree.

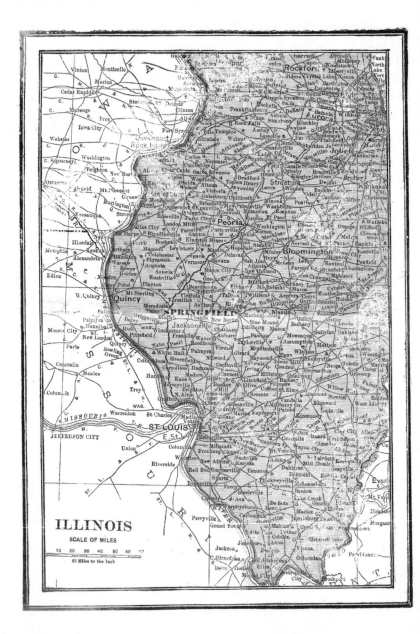

ILLINOIS

SCALE OF MILES

10 20 30 40 50 60 70

65 Miles to the Inch

CHAPTER SEVEN

CAPITAL PUNISHMENT

BY FATHER DEMETRI C. KANTZAVELOS

"EVERY HUMAN BEING IS WORTH MORE THAN
THE WORST THING THEY'VE DONE. ALL LIFE
HAS DIGNITY—GUILTY LIFE TOO."
—SISTER HELEN PREJEAN

I met the "monstrous" Andrew Kokoraleis at the Pontiac
Correctional Institution of Illinois just weeks before his scheduled
execution. Although I had visited inmates before, this was the first
time I was to meet someone on death row. After meeting the prison
personnel and enduring a body search, I passed through several
gates, which seemed to slam out the world behind. I was then taken
to a cold, concrete visiting room and was instructed to sit in one of
four chairs around a bare table. Everything was bolted to the floor.
Andrew, with his hands shackled together, was escorted to my table
by a guard.

Instead of encountering the monster this convicted murderer was said to be, I found him to be a person of great faith, at peace with himself as well as with his accusers. Indeed, he had been a criminal, a misfit who had wasted much of his time in this world. Yet for all of the seventeen years he had been imprisoned, Andrew had maintained his innocence of murder.

On the basis of that first visit, and many other direct experiences I had with him, I firmly believe that he was indeed innocent of this one crime for which he was ultimately killed. I cannot communicate to you what it felt like to have bonded so deeply with a person who had spent all of his adult life imprisoned. It was a strange, new experience for me. I was not naïve, but I was moved.

DONATE
Find an anti-death penalty organization or prison ministry and make a donation.

Nor can I describe what it felt like to have seen Christ face to face in prison, shackled, alone, with no family or friends. His only remaining family was his Greek Orthodox Church, which stood by his side as his family and galvanized the wider religious community in the face of the great social evil of capital punishment. We felt it incumbent upon ourselves to stand decisively for clemency for Andrew. Even though our pleas fell upon insensitive and even deaf political ears, we knew that we had to do what was Christlike.

And we tried—with letters, with demonstrations, with all the moral authority we could bring to bear. We publicized the fact that not a single shred of physical or scientific evidence existed that tied Andrew to the crime for which he was to be executed— no fingerprints, no DNA, no eye witnesses. In fact, the only evidence against him was a confession obtained by lengthy police interrogation that Andrew almost instantly recanted.

As the fatal day of his execution approached, we gathered many religious leaders in the Greek Orthodox Cathedral to offer the governor of Illinois our collective wisdom and prayers in his struggle. Former Governor Ryan turned a deaf ear to the religious community in general and in particular to the religious community of which Andrew was a part.

On March 17, 1999, our brother in Christ, Andrew Kokoraleis, was put to death by the state of Illinois. Two days later I returned home from an emotionally draining and difficult day at my office and received a letter from Andrew in the mail. With great care I opened the envelope and read the enclosed card. He told me that he hoped the death penalty would be abolished, and I absorbed every word into my being. I took what Andrew told me to heart, and I clearly heard his every word as a personal calling. His correspondence gratefully asked and hoped that by his execution, somehow, others might be spared a similar fate and that all executions might be terminated. He thanked me for the support I had provided him and told me that we would certainly see each other again in the kingdom of heaven.

Shortly following, the governor—under obvious political pressure and mired in a statewide scandal—announced a moratorium on executions in Illinois, which still stands today. The pressure to do so was enormous. Seventeen convicted criminals in our state awaiting execution had been vindicated and proven innocent of the crimes for which they were condemned. This was not achieved by the legal system "fixing" itself and serving justice. The innocence of these men was demonstrated mainly by a group of students in law school, reporters of the major newspapers, concerned relatives, and the many friends of the religious communities of our state and member organizations of the Illinois Coalition to Abolish the Death Penalty.

Brought to light for all to see was the truly "blind justice" of the broken system, which allowed these innocent men to be condemned: over-zealous police eager to find someone to blame for shocking crimes; eager prosecutors concerned with their win/loss statistics in order to advance their careers; cowardly politicians who did not want to appear "soft on crime" and who would rather allow innocent men to die than lose an election; and finally, a populace that, in the face of violence and horror in their neighborhoods, thirsted for vengeance—someone needed to be blamed! The murderer had to pay his debt to society.

But there was no payment. As Professor Richard Stith of Valparaiso University has put so succinctly, capital punishment "doesn't pay a debt; it kills the debtor."

THE REALITIES OF CAPITAL PUNISHMENT

Capital punishment is a reality in our world, one that I hope will change. This hope is based on my conviction that all human life is sacred, at every stage, in every circumstance—even the worst of circumstances. I believe that God loves the world and, despite our sinfulness, does not condemn us (John 3:16-17). I believe God wants us to love as He loves—even when that is hard for us, most especially when it appears impossible. It is possible, although very difficult, to "love your enemies," especially when they have committed the most horrific crimes against you, your loved ones, or your neighbors.

I am both a Christian and an American citizen who loves my country. Because of this, I am also an activist seeking to change the unfortunate reality of capital punishment in our world, our nation, and many of our states. I am not alone. There are many citizens, Christians and persons of other faith traditions, who share my hope. I stand with people from all walks of life, of every age, race, and belief. Through the moratorium on all executions in the state of Illinois, put in place by Governor Ryan in 2000, we effected change in Illinois with small steps and big hearts. But there is more to be done throughout our nation and our world.

The United States is one of the few countries in the world that executes criminals. For an all-too-brief time in this country we abolished the death penalty (1972-1977), but then we brought it back. Most nations have eliminated the death penalty as a violation of fundamental human rights. According to Amnesty International, 97 percent of all known executions in 2004 took place in

EDUCATE
Read *Dead Man Walking* and *The Death of Innocents* by Sister Helen Prejean or watch the documentary *Deadline.* Learn the facts about capital punishment.

four countries: China, Iran, Vietnam, and the United States. The United States routinely criticizes these very nations for their record on human rights. Our government protests vigorously when other nations prohibit religious freedom and political speech and institutionalize prejudice against minorities. It is very concerned with the rights of the citizens of the world, but not the right to life—officially accepting that a human being can forfeit his or her children's rights to live (through abortion) and that the government can take lives (through execution). Our government is deaf to most of the world when they criticize us for the state-sanctioned killing of our own citizens. Even Russia—notorious for human-rights violations and the slaughter of millions of its own citizens in the Soviet era spanning the majority of the twentieth century—has banned capital punishment among the many sudden, though incomplete, reforms in their society.

THE LIMITS OF WORLDLY JUSTICE

One of the hallmarks of civilized society is justice. In theory, capital punishment is the ultimate penalty imposed by society for the protection of its citizens. It has been around since prehistoric times. There is certain logic to "eye for eye, tooth for tooth." Capital punishment seeks to carry this logic to "life for life." The problem with this is that justice is delivered by human beings who are not always logical. Indeed, in our nation and others, the standard for the death penalty is "life for life," but includes other, non-murder crimes as well. Treason is one such example, but around the world, the punishment encompasses lesser crimes like sex outside of marriage.

We are not always absolutely certain about the guilt of those condemned to die; "beyond a reasonable doubt" is the standard for our nation, but this is not the same as certainty or "beyond all doubt." Unfortunately, some nations do not have legal systems as sophisticated or careful as our own. This means innocent human beings can be executed wherever capital punishment is the law of the land. Yet researchers have conclusively shown that in the United States alone, twenty innocent persons have been put to death since the beginning of the twentieth century. The number would likely be higher if there were more records and if modern forensic investigation had been available at an earlier date.

Innocent persons executed—this is not justice.

Human beings can be corrupt and seek the "legal" death of

someone for their own gain, even under the guise of the legal system. False accusations and witnesses are not uncommon. While most officers of the court may be well-meaning, sometimes unsavory characters seek to be police officers, attorneys, and judges. Sometimes politicians play on the fears of voters and promise to put an end to crime by killing the killers; political figures often pander to public whims. Sometimes people fear for their lives and react emotionally to crimes by demanding the death of those they suspect of being a threat to society, without knowing all the facts.

In short, the main problem with capital punishment is that innocent persons can be put to death. Not everyone agrees how we should avoid this. Some people still maintain that we can avoid it while continuing to execute criminals, but the evidence is just not on their side.

People have been convicted of capital crimes on the basis of coerced confessions; when this has been proven, some—not all—have been set free. People have been condemned following trials where their attorney was literally sleeping in court. Others have been sentenced to die despite the obvious incompetence and inexperience of their attorney. In Illinois, seventeen persons have been set free after long prison stays and numerous unsuccessful appeals. This occurred not because the legal system worked, but because concerned citizens outside the normal channels managed to show that the system was seriously flawed and proved beyond all doubt the innocence of the men in question.

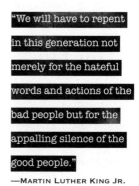

"We will have to repent in this generation not merely for the hateful words and actions of the bad people but for the appalling silence of the good people."

—MARTIN LUTHER KING JR.

The difficulty in preventing the innocent from being executed is not the only problem. Our system has many flaws, and one is the arbitrary sentencing to death of convicted criminals. Not all persons guilty of capital crimes are sentenced to die. What determines each individual's fate? People do. Politicians, for example, write the laws. I have already noted the problem with politicians in regard to making public policy. Prosecutors also play a role: sometimes they ask for the death penalty, sometimes not, depending on each particular situation or their career. Then there are the judges and juries. Along the way, individuals make choices based on their experiences, emotions, and prejudices. For example, minorities, the mentally impaired, and the poor are sentenced to die at a far greater rate than persons convicted for similar crimes among the majority, the intelligent, and the wealthy. It also depends on the location of the trial. Some states execute criminals; others do not. In some counties, prosecutors or judges will give death sentences; others, as a personal policy, will not. This is not "blind justice."

THE ETHICS OF CAPITAL PUNISHMENT

But there is more. There is a deeper, more serious problem than a flawed legal system: ethics. Is capital crime good for society? In theory, capital punishment is a deterrent to crime. In practice, it is not. There is no statistical evidence to show that the death penalty prevents crime. In fact, the opposite is true. In the United States, capital crimes are more common in states that have the death penalty and less common in states that do not have it.

But this does not really prove anything; maybe states adopted the death penalty because the crime problem was worse. However, in Canada, capital and violent crimes dropped 20 percent following the abolishment of the death penalty. Indeed, an argument from statistics could suggest that capital punishment actually increases violent crime!

The unjust killing of innocent persons can never be considered good for society. But if guilt was certain and beyond all doubt, could capital punishment be considered "good"?

Apparently the Russians do not think so, and the reasoning of one government spokesperson is worth repeating: "The abolition of capital punishment ... is aimed more at shaping the children's mentality—they will learn to live in a country where the State does not kill its own." The use of capital punishment by any society illustrates a value placed by that society on the life of its citizens. Laws are a guide for civil conduct. A law permitting the killing of a human being suggests that, under certain conditions, killing is a good thing. The Russians do not want their children to believe that. A portion of American society does believe that, as do other societies such as China, which also mandates infanticide to control its population size.

ACTIVATE

• Get involved with a local prison ministry.

• Become a pen pal with someone in jail.

• Go to a peaceful protest of an execution and pray.

• Lobby your local and state representatives to take a stand against the death penalty.

Some believe it better to kill the most violent criminals rather than support them in prison with tax money. Unfortunately, in the United States it costs taxpayers far more money, on average, to execute someone than to imprison him for forty years—a lifetime sentence for most prisoners. When those who support the death penalty learn this while responding to opinion polls, most prefer life imprisonment without possibility of parole to capital punishment. So much for principle!

CAPITAL PUNISHMENT AND THE CHURCH

When considering what is good for society, people naturally base their judgments on what is personally best for themselves. In a democracy such as the United States, this is how social policy is generally made—by the consensus of the majority. Still, it comes down to the personal beliefs of individual persons.

I oppose the death penalty, and I do so based on my beliefs regarding the good of our society. I actively seek to have capital punishment abolished, to reduce crime and general suffering in our society, which both results from crime and causes it. I do so not only because I am a concerned citizen, but because I am a person of faith.

Not all persons devoted to faith traditions oppose capital punishment, and not all Christians today oppose it, though a majority of Christians in the United States have serious issues with it as it is currently practiced. Be that as it may, in addition to the arguments above, I am convinced that capital punishment is ultimately inconsistent with the teachings of Jesus Christ, and this motivates me to share my belief. This is not to say that I believe my view should be imposed. It means I hope to convince my neighbors to rid the world of what I perceive to be an evil in our society.

Certainly the Old Testament, revered by Christians and Jews, prescribes capital punishment for some violations of the Law given to Moses. Yet many adherents of Judaism today oppose capital punishment on moral and theological grounds, and such internal debate is not limited to Christians and Jews. Christians generally interpret the Hebrew Scriptures in light of the New Testament and the teaching of Jesus. One verse seems to have particular bearing on the matter: "You have heard that it was said, 'Eye for eye, and tooth for tooth.' But I tell you, Do not resist an evil person. If someone strikes you on the right cheek, turn to him the other also" (Matt. 5:38-39, NIV). I do not believe that Jesus would suggest that violent criminals be allowed to inflict damage at will upon society, but His words suggest that there is another option to capital punishment.

I do not believe that convicted criminals are all innocent. But I do believe that life incarceration is a more humane punishment for all of us—the punished and the punishers. In the United States, "we the people" are ultimately the punishers. I do not want to be responsible for anyone's death—but I also do not wish for criminals to kill others. If they can be rehabilitated, this is a worthy cause to attempt, but prison culture often precludes this. However, prisoners have the ability to repent and come to faith and salvation. The Church can minister to living persons, corrupted as they may be. But the Church cannot call the dead to repentance and cannot visit and minister to them as Jesus taught.

> "You have heard that it was said, 'Eye for eye, and tooth for tooth.' But I tell you, do not resist an evil person. If anyone slaps you on the right cheek, turn to them the other cheek also."
>
> —MATTHEW 5:38-39, TNIV

During a recent interview, a radio personality in Chicago asked me a most interesting and important question: "What business does the Church have involving itself in issues like the death penalty?"

Calmly, I replied, "We are simply reclaiming our historic role." However, I might have answered: What business did the Hebrew

PRAY

Lord, although it was once said that a just punishment for crime was determined by the rule "eye for eye, tooth for tooth," when Christ came to abolish death by dying on the cross and being raised from the dead, we believe that He also gave a chance to all humans, male and female, slave and free, guilty and innocent to repent and be saved. To the repentant thief on the cross, Christ said, "Today you will be with me in paradise" (Luke 23:43, TNIV). We pray that those imprisoned for murder or other heinous crimes be given until the end of their natural lives to turn to You in love and be transformed. And we pray that any innocent people who have been imprisoned due to racism, classism, or for some other unjust reason be exonerated and given a chance to serve You in freedom. For You are a forgiving God who forgives all of our sins, and we glorify You. Amen.

prophets have involving themselves in the unjust treatment of orphans and widows? What business did the apostle Paul have decrying partiality and discrimination? What business did Saint Nicholas (popularly known as Santa Claus) have advocating for those condemned to death before the fury of the Roman emperor?

The answer, of course, is that it is the business of all Christians to respond to Christ, as He is found in the needs of "the least of these brothers of mine" (Matt. 25:40, NIV). Too often, Christians are tempted to forget this teaching of Jesus, or explain it away: "'Lord, when did we see you hungry or thirsty or a stranger or needing clothes or sick or in prison, and did not help you?' He will reply, 'I tell you the truth, whatever you did not do for one of the least of these, you did not do for me'" (Matt. 25:44-45, NIV). The apostle Paul tells us "if one part [of the body] suffers, every part suffers with it" (1 Cor. 12:26, NIV). This is as true for our "body politic" as it is for the Church.

The many ills of society—warfare and hatred, racial and ethnic intolerance, capital punishment, and others—afflict the entire human family, for all human beings are created in the image and likeness of God (Gen. 1:26). We are all surrounded by these evils. The scandal of their existence is not that humans are fallible—it is our failure to redress these wrongs. It is an almost universal truth: religious and moral teachings demand a higher standard of human and humane interactions. Each social ill is, in fact, an invitation to spiritual renewal, an opportunity to make compassion, humility, and fervent prayer the hallmarks of our humanity once again. Even when—or perhaps especially when—one of these ills does not affect our own community directly, the call to help is still there.

The question that we must ask ourselves is how willing we are to proclaim love in the face of hate for our neighbors and for the strangers in our midst. It is easy to be compassionate and reach out to those whom we know and love and who are most like us, but it is when we reach out to those whom we do not know, those who are unlike us, that we are living out the Gospel's message of love.

Never is this truer than when we encounter the human face of capital punishment. For people of faith, understanding and being one with a person who has been convicted of heinous crimes against helpless victims is an enormous challenge.

Every human being is created in the image and likeness of God. We are each an icon, an image of Christ, and a mirror to one another of God's living presence in the world. No human being is a "monster." And every human being, including Andrew Kokoraleis and every other death-row inmate, is of value and worth. This is true even for those who seem most evil—this mystery is perhaps the ultimate challenge of faith.

This is not as outrageous as it may sound at first. People of faith cannot, in good conscience, divide humans into categories of any kind. We risk the spiritual hypocrisy of intellectually convenient excuses for our in-activism.

WHAT YOU CAN DO

Not long before His own execution, Christ spoke these words of warning to all religious people: "Woe to you ... you hypocrites! You give a tenth of your spices ... but you have neglected the more important matters of the law—justice, mercy and faithfulness. You should have practiced the latter, without neglecting the former" (Matt. 23:23, NIV). We cannot ignore the evil of murder in any form, whether or not it is sanctioned by the state. We are called to action.

There are many ways to be active in seeking to eradicate the evil of capital punishment. For Christians, the first act is prayer—for the wisdom of our leaders to change our society for the better; for the safety of all; and for those imprisoned, that they would come to repentance and salvation. You can easily discuss the matter with friends and family. You can learn more—the Internet in particular is full of excellent sources on capital punishment. Pass on what you learn to the person next to you. Vote wisely. Become active in an organization that advocates the abolition of capital punishment, volunteering time and talent. And if you are a member of a faith community, ask your leaders what needs to be done. If they are not doing anything, encourage them! And remember:

Rather than righting the wrong of murder by convicting the guilty, the death penalty can and does send the innocent to death row.

Rather than executing only "the worst of the worst," the death penalty is imposed upon the poorest, the darkest-skinned, and the most shoddily represented among us.

Rather than saving the state the expense of life imprisonment, the death penalty costs more, at least three times as much.

Rather than serving as a deterrent, states with the death penalty have higher homicide and overall crime rates.

Rather than giving families of victims any kind of true closure, the death penalty forces them to obsess on vengeance, to continuously open old wounds. It draws them into the sinfulness of complicity in murder. Blood-lust is blood-guilt.

And finally, rather than addressing the complex social problems that provoke violent crime in the first place, the death penalty actually contributes to the worsening climate of violence.

That should not be what we want for our children. We need a culture of life, not death. We must actively seek this. In our activity, death shall have no dominion.

FATHER DEMETRI KANTZAVELOS is the chancellor of the Greek Orthodox Metropolis of Chicago. With an unyielding commitment to the sanctity of life, he is a well-known activist and advocate for social justice in the Midwest. He is the recent two-term president (2003-2005) of the Illinois Coalition to Abolish the Death Penalty and was the spiritual advisor to the last person executed in the state of Illinois, Andrew Kokoraleis.

AUTHOR'S NOTE:
The author is grateful to the Illinois Coalition to Abolish the Death Penalty as the source of facts for this article, which can be found at its website, *http://www.icadp. org/page7.html* (accessed August 31, 2005).

TURKISH ASIA,
ARABIA
AND
PERSIA
SCALE OF MILES

CHAPTER EIGHT

WAR AND PEACE

BY ROSE MARIE BERGER

"WAR MAY SOMETIMES BE A NECESSARY EVIL. BUT NO MATTER HOW NECESSARY, IT IS ALWAYS AN EVIL, NEVER A GOOD. WE WILL NOT LEARN HOW TO LIVE TOGETHER IN PEACE BY KILLING EACH OTHER'S CHILDREN."
—JIMMY CARTER

I was in a crowded lecture hall filled with Capitol Hill wonks. Palestinian diplomat Hanan Ashrawi addressed the gaggle on how new political solutions to the Israeli-Palestinian conflict must be embraced, or there would never be a just peace in Iraq or the "Muslim world." Ashrawi is an Anglican Christian, a feminist, author, poet, diplomat, and brave proponent of nonviolent resistance. She concluded with a phrase that has stayed with me. "Everyone knows what kind of war the United States can make. We long to see what kind of peace the United States can make."

I paraphrase her comment now to address the issue of Christians and war and peace. Everyone knows what kind of "war" Christians can make. Examples abound: the Crusades, the Inquisition, the pogroms against Jews, the Christian Church's alliance with Nazism and complicity in the death camps, the genocide in Bosnia, to name a few. Yet we long to see what kind of peace Christians can make.

I've spent most of my life around Christians experimenting with Gospel-based nonviolence, conflict resolution, and applied or pragmatic peacemaking. Some are involved in the systematic study of these. Most simply did what the situation required. Some called themselves Christian pacifists. Others had never heard of pacifism or rejected the label as weak. Some identified themselves as part of "God's Army," soldiers who carry no weapon but the cross. Some were conscientious objectors, refusing to serve as agents of death for the state or government. Some were military leaders who used violence only as a last resort. Others served their country militarily, but fought nonviolently against that same country's violent segregation laws.

Much has been written about Christians and war. There is much more to learn about Christians and peace.

WARMONGERS VERSUS PEACENIKS

In Monty Python's classic send-up of the life of Jesus (*The Life of Brian*, 1979), the Beatitudes in Matthew 5 are presented with great authenticity and sincerity. The comedy begins when members of the crowd mishear Jesus' statement, "Blessed are the peacemakers ..."

"I think he said, 'Blessed are the cheese makers,'" someone clarifies. "What's so special about the cheese makers?" a woman asks. "Well, obviously, this is not meant to be taken literally," her husband responds. "It refers to any manufacturers of dairy products."

This contemporary spoof isn't too far off from the Church's history on issues of war and peace. People hear what they want to hear or what someone else interprets for them, and then misapply it to their specific situation. Too often religion has added fuel to an already-enflamed debate and intensified already-polarized arguments between extremes. Churches allow the language of "warmongers" and "hawks" or "peaceniks" and "doves" to divide us down the middle, instead of allowing the Gospel to open a path for us in times of crisis.

DONATE
Give money to a
pacifist organization
of your choice.

As followers of Jesus, all we can do is continue returning to the original text and allow it to illuminate our contemporary questions, while keeping in mind all the filters of translation, theology, and context that may clarify or cloud it.

When Jesus said, "Blessed are the peacemakers, for they will be called children of God" (Matt. 5:9, TNIV), what did He mean? Or when He said, "If anyone slaps you on the right cheek, turn to them the other cheek also. And if anyone wants to sue you and take your shirt, hand over your coat as well" (Matt. 5:39-40, TNIV)? Or "Love your enemies, and pray for those who persecute you" (Matt. 5:44, TNIV)?

These texts and others, plus the living memory of how Jesus and the disciples acted, caused early generations of Christians to refuse to participate in war (those who did were counseled and sometimes asked not to participate in communion for a period of time, although they were not completely cut off from community). Soldiers who subsequently converted to Christianity often left military service, viewing it as incompatible with their new life. Why? Largely because of idolatry. Military service forced them to put the gods of nationalism ahead of the God of Jesus Christ. Military service also fostered hatred for an enemy, an attitude viewed as antithetical to Christ's teachings. "Love of enemies is the principal precept of the Christian," said the Tunisian theologian Tertullian in the first century. Until the time of Constantine, no Christian writing allowed for Christians to participate in war. Military valor was not a virtue. True victory was won through love.

The phrase "Christian peacemakers" might be considered redundant. Christians, by the very nature of Christ's call on our lives, prioritize peace with justice and reject violence in all its forms. We are the experimenters of a new paradigm. As Roland Bainton, Reformation scholar and professor of church history, wrote, "Christianity brings to social problems, not a detailed code of ethics or a new political theory, but a new scale of values."[1] Christians, then, are those who examine inevitable human conflict through the lens of a "new scale of values." We don't settle for the old formulas. We are called to be courageous innovators who defend the "least of these"—without the benefit of the world's weapons.

> "Wisdom is better than weapons of war."
> —ECCLESIASTES 9:18, TNIV

If Christians are to live a new scale of values, we must ask what those values are. The first is love. Jesus summarized all the teachings as "Love God and love your neighbor." Our neighbor, we know, isn't just found in our family, workplace, or apartment. It's the kid flashing gang signs, the smelly homeless man who lives in the park, the transgender prostitute who works the downtown corner, the crazy old woman who lives alone outside of town, and the immigrant family that doesn't speak English and always seems angry. Jesus gives us the strength of God's love so that we can learn to be allies with those whom society has pushed to the margins.

But Jesus doesn't leave us with loving our neighbor. If I preach on Sunday morning about those that the church helps, if I say, in effect, "See! We love poor people because we have a low-income housing project and a clothing donation box. We love the hungry because we have a soup kitchen. We love unwed mothers because we support an adoption service and provide counseling," then the congregation will say what a good Christian I am and shower me with "God bless you."

But if I follow Jesus' instruction to "love your enemies," praise from the congregation lessens just a bit.

If I add, "See! We love Iraqis and provide medical supplies for them. We love Muslims and are part of a Qur'an study. We love gang members and meet with them for counseling. We've loved the families of suicide bombers and heard their anguish. We love dictators and have met with members of their governments. We love torturers, husbands who beat their wives, rapists, and pedophiles and have prayed with them," not only has the praise died to silence, but I'll be lucky if I get out of the church in one piece. No wonder the crowds wanted to toss Jesus off the cliff!

This Christian love that we profess and strive toward must be strong enough to engage even these enemies, or it is nothing but a "sounding gong." Not, of course, that we endorse such horrible acts of injustice, but there is no room in the Christian life for only associating with certain kinds of people. Everything that Jesus did and that the early Church carried on after Him was about embracing the unembraceable and breaking down walls of division. The nature of another's sin cannot—with God's grace—be a barrier to our love for him or her.

This precept—love of enemies—is one of the unique aspects of our life in Christ. Other religions care for the poor and promote justice. Few prioritize love of enemies. In some ways, that was why Jesus said, "Let any one of you who is without sin be the first to throw a stone at her" (John 8:7, TNIV). It's not just to reveal the hypocrisy of the judgers or to show mercy to the accused; it's also to enable the accusers to love the accused. The apostle Paul constantly reminded us of our sinfulness and our salvation as sinners, not because he wanted us to feel bad about ourselves, but because recognition of our own sinfulness creates in us the capacity to see beyond the sins of others.

'I HAVE NOT COME TO BRING PEACE, BUT THE SWORD'

But we must ask the question: Does the New Testament approve of war in some cases? What about the military images in the Gospels and the epistles? Let's take a quick look at the verses most often used to challenge the gospel of peace: "Jesus entered the temple courts and began driving out those who were buying and selling there. He overturned the tables of the moneychangers and the benches of those selling doves" (Mark 11:15, TNIV).

Does this prove that Jesus used violence in pursuit of God's justice? Like Jesus, should we drive terrorists out by violence if necessary to defend the weak and protect God's justice?

Every Christian is charged with resisting evil, but none are given the right to kill. Jesus did not kill anyone, nor threaten to kill anyone if he or she didn't follow His command. His strength and persuasion were in His spiritual authority, not His acts of violence.

"The outer court of the temple ..." wrote Richard McSorley, co-founder of the pacifist group Pax Christi USA, in *New Testament Basis of Peacemaking*, "was the only place Gentiles were allowed for prayer. By closing it off from Gentile use, [the marketers] were nationalizing the temple, including only Jews. By His action, Jesus was insisting that the temple be open to all ..."[2]

"I did not come to bring peace, but a sword" (Matt. 10:34, TNIV).

Is Jesus saying that the kingdom will be established by violence if necessary?

"Peace" in this verse refers to that weak creature that develops through submission and fear, not the deep peace of Christ rooted in righteousness and justice. Conversely, "sword" in this verse is a metaphor for the Word of God that cuts through the gauze of worldly custom—a sword to prick the conscience, a choice that must be made to take up the cross of Christ.

In Church Father John Chrysostom's homily on Matthew 10:34, he likens the sword spoken of in this verse to the knife wielded by a physician removing a deadly growth: "This more than anything is peace, when the diseased is cut off, when the mutinous is removed. For thus it is possible for heaven to be united to earth. Since the physician too in this way preserves the rest of the body, when he amputates the incurable part."[3]

"And if you don't have a sword, sell your cloak and buy one" (Luke 22:36, TNIV).

Why would Jesus tell someone to buy a sword if He didn't

EDUCATE
Learn about current wars being waged around the world and the issues surrounding them. Thoughtfully engage others in peaceful dialogues about how violence might be avoided.

intend for them to use it? Isn't Jesus giving His disciples the "right to bear arms"?

In Isaiah 53, there is a reference to the suffering Servant. Jesus could have intended for the sword to be used symbolically, to fulfill the description in Isaiah 53:12 that says the Servant will be "numbered with the transgressors." It was illegal for Jews to carry weapons under the Roman occupation. "It appears that on this one specific occasion Jesus deliberately arranged for his disciples to be in possession of weapons," wrote Presbyterian minister Rob Yule, "so that even though he was not a criminal, he might be arrested as one."[4] However, it seems like Jesus' intention was not for the weapons to be used to protect or defend Him because a few verses later he rebuked Peter for using the sword.

This brief look at a few controversial verses only indicates that there are levels of interpretation of Scripture. Our understanding of Scripture cannot only be skin-deep. God invites us to plunge into the depths of the Word, examining the content in which each book of the Bible was written and soaking ourselves in its healing and dangerous waters.

IF NOT US, THEN WHO?

As Christians, we believe Jesus gave us the Holy Spirit so that we could take on a spirit of love, not fear. We are uniquely called to live our lives as peacemakers, and we have been given special gifts to accomplish this difficult task. Saint Basil preached, "I cannot persuade myself that without love to others, and without, as far as rests with me, peaceableness towards all, I can be called a worthy servant of Jesus Christ." Saint John Chrysostom compares Christians to children suckling the milk of peace from the breast of Christ.

As I said earlier, I've spent most of my life immersed in the stories and reflections of Christians experimenting with Gospel-based nonviolence, conflict resolution, and applied or pragmatic peacemaking. These are ordinary people who rely on God and their spiritual disciplines and teachings to develop brave and creative responses in situations of violence or injustice. These are the people of the Third Way. They refuse to identify others as "enemies" and instead direct themselves to the root causes of injustice.

I use the word "experimenting" the way Gandhi used it when he said that our lives are "experiments in truth" and we are scientists testing, probing, analyzing, and drawing conclusions based on those experiments. Gandhi's goal was to "see God face to face."[5] The use of the word "experiment" encourages flexibility and creativity, rather than rigid dogmatism. The people I've met are indeed "experimenting" with how the gospel of peace applies in a certain situation. Catholic Worker founder Dorothy Day described her movement in a similar fashion. "I thought we were creating a community," she said, "but the Catholic Worker turned out to be more of a school." A place for testing Christian values, for experimenting with the Gospel, a place for discipling.

LOVE YOUR ENEMIES

One of the "new scale of values" mentioned by Roland Bainton in *Christian Attitudes Toward War and Peace* is assuming an attitude of love and concern for the well-being of one's enemy. For example, in June 1992 Serb paramilitaries invaded the Franciscan Theological School in Sarajevo, holding everyone inside prisoner. There were sixteen Catholic priests and brothers and eight nuns. The soldiers were very amped up, some buzzing on cocaine. They were going through the school, destroying everything: shooting up the chapel, ripping the paintings off the walls, burning the library, hitting the priests with rifle butts. The captives were certain that any minute they would be murdered.

In the midst of horrific chaos, a priest told me later, he remembered a remarkable exchange. Sister Isadora, in her eighties, addressed the young militants with love, "like they were her grandsons." One man, barely in his twenties, had blood and brain matter spattered across his shirt. He was trying to ignore it, but it clearly bothered him, and he kept trying to wipe it off. "My boy," said Sister Isadora, "please, your shirt is stained. Let me get some water and clean it." She took a damp rag and began to carefully clean the blood from his collar. When she finished, she asked to go to the bathroom to clean off the rag. The young man and one of the priests accompanied her. When they returned, the soldier had his gun pressed hard into the priest's side. Sister Isadora touched the man's arm and waved the gun away. "Move that out of the way," she said. "Come with me and let us go to the kitchen and make some tea." And so he did. When the soldier's superiors found out, they were very angry, but that young soldier never harmed the captives. After several days a prisoner exchange was negotiated, and the priests and nuns were released. None of them were killed.

> "No act of kindness, no matter how small, is ever wasted."
>
> —AESOP

In this example, human dignity, respect, and the power of all parties were emphasized. Enemies are created through a process of dehumanizing one side or another. Through Christ we are able to see each one as a child of God, created in God's image. This also means acknowledging our own fallenness and complicity in situations of violence. Sister Isadora made sure that both the "enemy" and the "victims" maintained their humanity.

TAKING THE INITIATIVE

Another key value is opening up space for dialogue through independent initiatives. In 1997, Catholics in the community of San Jose de Apartado, Colombia, were increasingly threatened by violence from the Colombian military, paramilitaries, drug cartels, and insurgents. Sixteen thousand people had been displaced, whole villages abandoned, community leaders assassinated. All of the armed actors (a term used to describe guerrilla fighters) claimed that the civilians were siding with the enemy—whoever that happened to be. Finally, the citizens of San Jose de Apartado, along with representatives from twenty-eight of the surrounding villages, asked for a meeting with their local Catholic bishop. They proposed to designate an area around their towns as a "neutral zone" in which civilians would be respected and protected.

The bishop brought the proposal to the Intercongregational Commission for Justice and Peace, which agreed to lead workshops through local churches to shape the idea and to train people in nonviolence. In March 1997 the Peace Community of San Jose de Apartado was established. All participants were expected to covenant to a set of ground rules: a) participate in community efforts, b) say "no" to injustice and impunity, c) do not participate directly or indirectly in the war, d) do not carry weapons, and e) do not manipulate or give information to any armed actors or their associates. Soon other religious peace groups began sending observers to the project. Their presence brought international attention and protection to the peace community experiment. As of 2001, more than twenty peace communities were established throughout northern Colombia. Pax Christi, an international

Catholic peace organization, says that the peace community model "allows displaced citizens of the region to autonomously reconstruct their lives in communities that are self-proclaimed zones of peace."

When I visited Colombia in 2001, each house in the peace communities flew a white flag to identify itself. Sadly, this model has not protected the citizens from violence. There have still been murders by the armed actors. Deals brokered with drug cartels and insurgents to respect the peace communities have occasionally been broken. But the violence has been greatly reduced, and most of the citizens are no longer displaced, but living in their own homes. This type of independent initiative can reduce violence and promote justice. A "third way" was opened that can break stalemates and create new space for dialogue.

ROOT OF THE PROBLEM

A third value is addressing the roots of a conflict, not just the symptoms. Brendan McAllister, director of The Mediation Network in Belfast, Northern Ireland, and a member of the Protestant and Catholic peace community called Corrymeela, has spent years trying to get Protestants and Catholics to stop killing each other. In his conversations with those on both sides, he quickly learned that most of the killing was motivated by revenge. But it went even deeper than retaliation. "One young man whose brother had been beaten to death told me that if he didn't go after the ones who killed his brother, it would be like his brother's life didn't matter," McAllister said. "They often feel that the only way to honor the dead is by taking another's life."

In response to this insight, members of The Mediation Network worked with local churches to establish public candlelight vigils whenever someone was killed. By developing rituals to address the deeper issue of grief and honor the memory of loved ones, they were able to reduce "revenge killings." Addressing the roots of a conflict requires wisdom, historical perspective, political action, and a pastoral gaze to recognize underlying wounds that may contribute to conflict.

NONVIOLENT PROTESTS

A fourth value is supporting nonviolent direct action, especially that which is relationally based. Thousands of stories from the American civil rights movement demonstrate friendships that arose across color lines and motivated action to promote and protect "liberty and justice for all." One story was told to me by a sixty-year-old prison guard named Geraldine. In the early 1960s, Geraldine—a working-class white woman from the Northwest— was stationed at Fort McClellan, Alabama, home of the Women's Army Corps. Geraldine's best friend in the corps was another enlisted woman from Chicago, called "Westy," who was African American. The week before Christmas in 1962 the two women decided to pursue their own strategy for promoting integration. They'd walk in the front door of restaurants throughout Alabama— a black woman and a white woman in full military uniform—and order lunch. They'd sit there until someone kicked them out. "We were thrown out of many places around Anniston and Selma and that area," recalls Geraldine. "We were in uniform because at that time we were not allowed civilian clothing while in basic training. But it really shook them up to see us in uniform. It took them a little longer to ask us to leave."

A few years later, in the spring of 1965, Geraldine was on her way to Virginia for duty when she learned of the ill-fated civil rights march that ended in severe beatings by the police at the Edmund

Pettis Bridge in Selma, Alabama. "I heard Dr. King was calling for a second march," Geraldine continued, "so I got hold of Westy, and we met up and marched together—only that time we were not in uniform." They joined the twenty-five thousand who arrived triumphantly in Montgomery on March 25, 1965. "It was amazing to be there," Geraldine told me, "but every face along the way was so filled with hate. The look of hate was the same then as it is today. I didn't understand racism then, and I don't understand it now. I am just so glad my three stepchildren were raised without prejudice."

VIOLENCE-REDUCING STRATEGIES

A fifth value: when a nonviolent strategy is not available, support strategies will produce measurable and immediate violence reduction, which then can create space for nonviolent initiatives. Sometimes violence-reduction strategies are the only option available, and they may be found in unlikely places. David Christie was a young Scottish soldier in the British peacekeeping forces in Yemen in the late 1960s. "The situation was similar to Iraq," Christie wrote in the South African magazine *Today*, "with people being killed every day. Not only were we tough, but we had the power to pretty well destroy the whole town had we wished."[6] But he had a commander who understood that their duty was to promote and build peace, and he trained his men to do something unusual: not to react when attacked.

"Only if we were 100 percent certain that a particular person had thrown a grenade or fired a shot at us were we allowed to fire," Christie wrote. "During our tour of duty we had 102 grenades thrown at us, and in response the battalion fired the grand total of two shots, killing one grenade-thrower. The cost to us was over one hundred of our own men wounded, and surely by the grace of God only one killed. When they threw rocks at us, we stood fast. When they threw grenades, we hit the deck and after the explosions we got to our feet and stood fast. We did not react in anger or indiscriminately. This was not the anticipated reaction. Slowly, very slowly, the local people began to trust us and made it clear to the local terrorists that they were not welcome in their area."

In the years since this pivotal experience, Christie has reflected biblically on violence-reduction strategies. "One way to stop the spiral of violence is highlighted in 2 Samuel 2:26-28, when Abner (Saul's commander) and Joab (David's commander) decided to stop fighting," Christie said. "In fact it was the unilateral decision of Joab, who was winning, to stop the war. He had his enemy at his mercy but forbore. There were still many problems thereafter, but the significant outcome was the reunification of Israel and Judah, ushering in the reign of King David. In fact, Israel had a regime change free of bloodshed when the armies stopped fighting."

Particularly for Christians, it is important to uphold the value of accepting responsibility for wrong actions and seeking repentance and forgiveness. In the powerful documentary *A Force More Powerful*, filmmaker Steve York interviews South African ANC (African National Congress) leader Mkhuseli Jack, as well as Lourens du Plessis, chief of police intelligence in the Eastern Cape

ACTIVATE

• Get involved with a pacifist organization.

• Participate in a peaceful antiwar protest.

• Show support of our troops by sending care packages and letters to soldiers.

• Contact your representatives and let them know how you feel about war.

PRAY

Lord, although the matter of war is complex, we know that You have created every person in Your image and likeness and have commanded us not to kill, saying that if we live by the sword, we die by the sword. If we are at war, Father, help our troops to cause a minimal amount of damage, and protect the innocent; if we are about to enter into a war, please help our leaders to take whatever measures necessary to avoid violence. And as for others who are at war, help the rift between the warring nations to be mended as quickly and as painlessly as possible. Help us to always strive to bring about peaceful ends to whatever conflicts come our way, and give us the strength to sacrifice ourselves for our brothers and sisters around the world and the humility to turn the other cheek to our enemies who strike us, whenever possible. Amen.

during the 1980s. When York first went to South Africa, he contacted Jack to ask if he knew any police or military officers who might be willing to be interviewed. Jack sent him to du Plessis. When York asked how to contact du Plessis, Jack said, "You have my phone number at work. He works for me now." Du Plessis, a white Afrikaner Christian, had been involved in horrific counter-insurgency programs in his position as head of police intelligence. However, unlike many of his colleagues, he complied when the South African Truth and Reconciliation Commission called him to testify. His testimony included evidence that directly linked officials in Pretoria to the assassination of three leading anti-apartheid activists— murders that had been a mystery for ten years. Du Plessis expressed deep remorse as he began to understand the results of his actions. After testifying, du Plessis was ostracized by whites and blacks alike. Only Jack approached him and acknowledged that du Plessis had suffered for his honesty and been insufficiently compensated for his testimony. Jack offered him a job in his construction company. Now the two are like brothers. "It takes my breath away," York said, "to see these men who have the wisdom, common sense, and broader vision to know that they must go forward together."[7]

These are just a few examples from individuals you may not have heard about before. But I encourage you to also read the stories of the lives of more famous Christians who have experimented with Jesus' call to peacemaking—Cesar Chavez, Dorothy Day, Martin Luther King Jr., Clarence Jordan, Dietrich Bonhoeffer, Oscar Romero, Dianna Ortiz, Fannie Lou Hamer, Albertina Sisulu, Hanan Ashrawi, Rachel Corrie, Dolores Huerta, Franz Jägerstätter, Martin Niemöller, Christophe Munzihirwa, Juan Gerardi, and Dorothy Stang, to name a few from the twentieth century.

The world longs to see the kind of peace Christians can make. We want to be about the business of disarming ourselves from that which divides and dominates—handguns, war, nuclear weapons, suicide bombs, mace, security systems, private defense contractors, private armies, bloated defense budgets. Instead, let's experiment with putting on the whole armor of God, as it says in Ephesians 6. Wrap truth around our waist and put on right action as our Kevlar vest. Lace up boots that prepare us to do the work of peace. Carry with us the defense system of our faith to protect us from the incoming missiles of sin. Put on the hardhat of God's wisdom and carry no weapon but the Word of God. Above all else, pray, pray, pray.

TEN PRACTICES OF 'JUST PEACEMAKING'[8]

1. Support nonviolent direct action.

2. Take independent initiatives to reduce threat.

3. Use cooperative conflict resolution.

4. Acknowledge responsibility for conflict and injustice and seek repentance and forgiveness.

5. Advance democracy, human rights, and religious liberty.

6. Foster just and sustainable economic development.

7. Work with emerging cooperative forces in the international system.

8. Strengthen the United Nations and international efforts for cooperation and human rights.

9. Reduce offensive weapons and weapons trade.

10. Encourage grassroots peacemaking groups and voluntary associations.

ROSE MARIE BERGER, an associate editor of Sojourners (*www.sojo.net*), is a Catholic peace activist and poet.

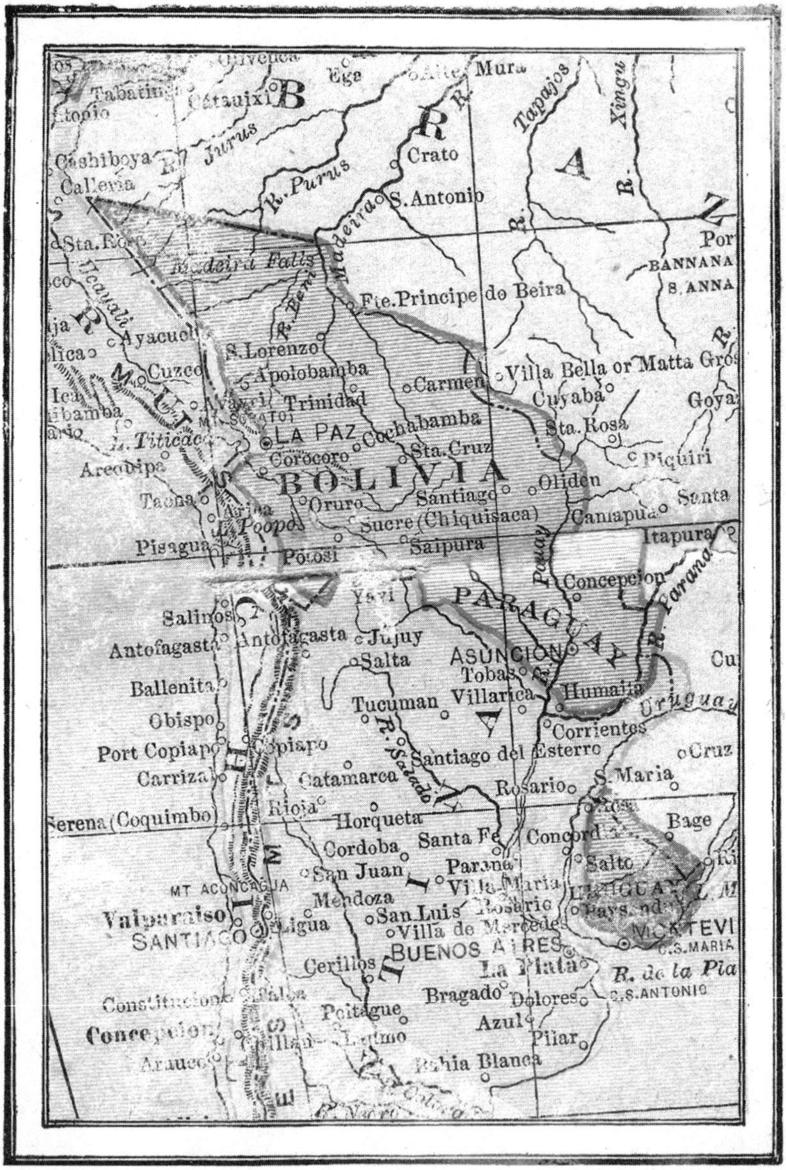

Ega
Mura
Tabatinga
Jurus
R. Purus
Crato
S. Antonio
Tapajos
Xingu
Madeira
Madeira Falls
Beni
Ucayali
Cashiboya
Sta. Rosa
Fte. Principe do Beira
BANNANA
S. ANNA
Ayacucho
Cuzco
S. Lorenzo
Apolobamba
Carmen
Villa Bella or Matta Grosso
Cuyaba
Trinidad
Goyaz
L. Titicaca
LA PAZ
Cochabamba
Sta. Rosa
Sta. Cruz
Corocoro
Piquiri
Arequipa
BOLIVIA
Oliden
Tacna
Oruro
Santiago
Santa
Sucre (Chiquisaca)
Camapua
Poopo
Pisagua
Potosi
Saipura
Itapura
Concepcion
PARAGUAY
Parana
Salinos
Antofagasta
Jujuy
Salta
ASUNCION
Tobas
Ballenita
Tucuman
Villarica
Humaita
Uruguay
Obispo
Corrientes
Port Copiapo
Copiapo
R. Salado
Santiago del Estero
Cruz
Carrizal
Catamarca
Rosario
S. Maria
Rioja
Serena (Coquimbo)
Horqueta
Bage
Santa Fe
Concord
Cordoba
Salto
San Juan
Parana
MT ACONCAGUA
Mendoza
Villa Maria
URUGUAY
Valparaiso
San Luis
Rosario
Paysandu
SANTIAGO
Ligua
Villa de Mercedes
BUENOS AIRES
C. S. MARIA
Cerillos
La Plata
R. de la Pla
Bragado
Dolores
C. S. ANTONIO
Constitucion
Talca
Poitague
Concepcion
Azul
Pilar
Arauco
Bahia Blanca

CHAPTER NINE

TORTURE

BY REAGAN DEMAS

"THE DEGREE OF CIVILIZATION IN A SOCIETY
CAN BY JUDGED BY ENTERING ITS PRISONS."
—FYODOR DOSTOEVSKY

I've never spent a night in prison. I'm guessing the same is true for you. It's hard to imagine what it would be like to be tossed into a cell and tortured for a crime I did not commit. After all, in the words of philosopher Immanuel Kant, "That all our knowledge begins with experience, there is indeed no doubt." There are so many things in life that are difficult to grasp until we actually live the experience or see with our own eyes.

So when I was first told that more than 130 countries around the world practice torture—defined under international law as the intentional infliction of severe mental or physical pain for a specific purpose—it was easy for my eyes to glaze over. It's just hard to compute a statistic like that. Learning that millions of individuals are being held in jail cells for lengthy periods of time in "remand"— that amorphous zone of incarceration used by governments worldwide to hold individuals prior to actually charging them with any alleged violation of the law—doesn't compel many of us to step away from our self-absorbed existences and leap into action. These are simply statistics.

But there are those for whom the statistics on torture resonate deeply. These are the individuals around the world who have personally suffered the inhuman indignity of flogging, sexual abuse, tooth extraction, limb amputation, castration, or any of the multitudinous mechanisms of torture used by governments and rebel groups worldwide to crush the human will.

THE FACES OF TORTURE

I can assure you that torture is much more than a statistic for David. David is a passionate twenty-four-year-old with a personality so large and warm it often completely hides the depth of suffering he has experienced in his youthful life. David was renting a video in a small East African town several years ago when a group of inebriated police officers decided to drag some local citizens to the police station and extract bribes from them. One officer asked David if he "had something" for them, and then told David to "bring it." David gave the officer the meager amount of money he had, and the officer let David go. But as David was walking out of the police compound, he heard three shots ring out and felt a sharp pain in his torso and right arm. The police officers had shot David from behind. Bleeding profusely, David managed to crawl to a nearby hospital. His wounds were so severe that doctors had to immediately amputate his arm.

Realizing that they had to cover up their crimes, the officers who had shot David entered the hospital and demanded that the hospital stop treating him. The doctors refused, so the officers shackled David to his hospital bed. As soon as he was released from the hospital, the police tossed David—who had committed no crime—into a squalid cell and charged him with the armed robbery of a nearby store, a crime which carries a mandatory sentence of death.

DONATE
Research different anti-torture missions and make a donation to one.

The statistic also resonates deeply with Adriana. At the age of seventeen, Adriana was living on the streets in Bolivia. She had stolen a leather jacket to keep warm with her friend, Maribel, when they were stopped by local police. The police took the two girls into the Andes Mountains, threw Adriana into a body of water, and passed an electric current through the water with an electric-shock weapon. They then forced Adriana to remove her clothes and beat her with their government-issued batons. Leaving Adriana lying naked in the snow, the police took Maribel further into the mountains. A bus driver stopped and picked up Adriana, saving her from death by exposure. But the vicious police beatings and shock torture had caused Adriana, who was pregnant, to lose her child. Maribel was never seen again.

There are those who say it's always hard to know the right thing to do. As Lyndon B. Johnson said, "Doing what is right is easy. The problem is knowing what is right." But we're not talking about the gray areas of life here. We're not talking about insignificant rights or debatable wrongs. We're talking about the arbitrary stripping away of the most basic of human rights—our freedom and dignity. This is injustice on a massive scale that would make even the staunchest relativist step off his soapbox.

Let's start with some basics about torture and abusive detention. Torture is condemned and forbidden in a number of international covenants, including the Convention against Torture or Other Cruel, Inhuman or Degrading Treatment or Punishment, which has been ratified by 136 countries. Each of these documents—including the African Charter on Human and Peoples' Rights, Article 7 of the International Covenant on Civil and Political Rights, Article 3 of the Geneva Conventions, and Article 5 of the Universal Declaration of Human Rights—affirm the right of every person to be free from cruel, inhuman, or degrading treatment. The prohibitions against torture apply to numerous abusive acts, including electric shock, near drowning, near suffocation, burning, whipping, use of needles under fingernails, mutilation, amputation, and hanging by hands or feet for prolonged periods.

> "If I can stop one heart from breaking, I shall not live in vain; If I can ease one life the aching, Or cool one pain, Or help one fainting robin Up to his nest again, I shall not live in vain."
>
> —EMILY DICKINSON

Often associated with acts of torture, abusive detention is any form of incarceration or restriction on an individual's freedom that does not comport with local or international law. This type of abuse includes the arrest and incarceration of an individual without being formally charged before a court of law within a legally specified time period, usually forty-eight hours. It also includes those instances where officials arbitrarily arrest and pursue false charges against individuals to cover up other acts of abuse.

Civil rights activist Martin Luther King Jr. also lived the statistic. He was arrested more than twenty times in his life. Indeed, it was from within the confines of a filthy jail cell, on the margins of a frayed newspaper editorial page, that King penned his "Letter from a Birmingham Jail"—a bold call for Christians to take an emphatic stance against the injustice of the segregated South. It was while King and his colleagues were being detained and abused in these jail cells that he wrote, "Injustice anywhere is a threat to justice everywhere. Whatever affects one directly, affects all indirectly."

In that way, these stories of unimaginable abuse have become our own stories.

King's call to Christian action still applies today. King and anti-apartheid leader Nelson Mandela (who spent twenty-seven years in a tiny South African jail cell) were two of the most vigorous crusaders for justice in the twentieth century. Both men, who led two justice movements on two continents, were fond of compelling others to action by noting that "the time is always right to do what is right."

Yet today, the scourge of abusive detention and torture continues to stain the fabric of human history. For those of us who do not live under the constant threat of having our freedom stripped away, the problem seems distant and the urgency unwarranted. But ask Samuel how distant the problem is. Samuel worked at a bank in an East African country. One day he showed up to work and was promptly arrested, accused of having held up the bank the day before. Samuel had done no such thing, but he was immediately put in a cell and charged with a crime that carried a mandatory penalty of death. The judge in Samuel's case paid him a visit in jail and asked Samuel to pay him some money in exchange for his release. Samuel refused. The police had no evidence that Samuel had committed the robbery, so in order to convict him they needed a confession. For weeks he was electrically shocked, humiliated, and bludgeoned. He never confessed, so he was held on false and inadequate evidence and spent almost three and a half years behind bars.

THE PRACTICE OF TORTURE

No country on earth publicly supports torture, and no country openly opposes its eradication. Ask anyone whether they condone the use of the rack on political prisoners or water torture on thieves to elicit confession, and the response will likely be a resounding "no." Nevertheless, Amnesty International reports that in 2004, forty-four countries on four continents held prisoners of conscience (people held for their beliefs), and fifty-eight countries arbitrarily arrested and detained individuals without charge or trial. The United States was one of them. If no country wants to admit that it practices torture and abusive detention, why are these so ubiquitous?

Abusive practices are prevalent because those with power in society, if left unrestrained, can too easily exercise that power to exploit those that are more vulnerable. Absolute power corrupts, absolutely, but any sort of unchecked power can corrupt. The dangers of power are curbed only by an established rule of law and accountability to that law enforced by a functional justice system. The temptation to exploit another for personal gain can be overwhelmingly strong when one knows he or she will actually get away with it.

It should come as no surprise that one West African nation would not admit to using a horsewhip or wooden roofing material or cable wire to beat prisoners. It makes sense that the United States would maintain its public opposition to torture even while attempting to craft an ambiguous policy regarding interrogation

144

techniques in the war on terror that seems intent upon preserving options indefensible in moral discourse. It's no wonder that another nation wouldn't dare concede the fact that 90 percent of detainees in one of its political detention facilities had been tortured by state agents. Abuses that are obviously wrong cannot be practiced wantonly by societies that do not wish to be branded as global pariahs. Suffocation by a plastic bag placed over the head is just not an acceptable form of human interaction. The use of pliers, pins, or shock treatment on the genitals isn't compatible with a civil society that respects human rights. Neither is the injection of drugs and serums to elicit confessions of dubious authenticity.

The very fact that these practices can occur only under the cover of darkness— behind denials, obfuscation, and official cover-up—is powerful evidence that the practices are indeed abusive and immoral. A young child who knocks over the cookie jar while sneaking a sweet before dinner must quickly hide the broken pieces of the jar because he knows he has done something wrong. And when his parents ask how the cookie jar was broken, the family cat will likely be blamed for the incident. In the same way, few countries admit the use of torture because it is simply impossible to make a non-frivolous argument for the morality of

EDUCATE
Read *The Blindfold's Eyes* by Sister Dianna Ortiz and the Geneva Convention (*www.enevaconventions.org*). Learn about those who have been tortured and share their stories with others. Putting a human face on the issue of torture will propel the anti-torture movement forward. Share the information with friends, acquaintances, colleagues, and elected officials.

the practice.

Nevertheless, these practices occur across the globe, on all continents, in developed and developing countries. You would think the fact that most countries have passed laws forbidding abusive detention and torture would be sufficient to end the abhorrent practices. But as Cervantes wrote in *Don Quixote*, "Laws go as Kings like." Laws and written edicts forbidding torture are little more than words on paper where there is no vigorous enforcement of the law. A security service agent may perceive little risk to himself in pistol-whipping a prisoner who refuses to confess to a crime. But his calculation will change dramatically the moment he learns that any state official found abusing a prisoner will be subject to immediate dismissal and public prosecution.

FIGHTING THE INJUSTICE OF TORTURE

You may be convinced that the world is an unjust place. So the response may be: How does this impact me? Are these really my problems? Abusive detention and torture are problems not only across oceans, but in our own backyards. The United States has been criticized by numerous human rights groups for its alleged use of abusive detention in the war on terror. The United States is party to a slew of conventions barring torture and speaks out against torture universally. But faced with alleged terrorist detainees, application of the spoken principle has proven to be an ethical challenge. The blanket condemnation begins to unravel when the "hard cases" arise, such as the need to extract a confession to prevent an impending act of terrorism.

A moral principle cannot waver in times of inconvenience. If torture and abusive detention are morally wrong, Christians cannot sit idly by simply because current circumstances make it more difficult to stand by what seemed like an obvious principle of right in times of greater convenience.

The living God of the universe doesn't waver on issues of principle, and neither should we. He cares unceasingly about the injustices of the world, including abusive detention and torture. If we truly believe that all humans are created in the image of God, we must also believe that they all are to be treated according to God's standards. While any sovereign state has the duty to detain, convict, and imprison perpetrators of crime, God's exhortations against abusive treatment of those created in His image do not cease to apply once an individual has violated the law. In fact, His biblical commandments specifically remind us that we are to treat prisoners—the very people we might brand most unworthy—with dignity and respect.

The Bible speaks in not-so-subtle terms about God's heart for those who suffer under abusive detention. Isaiah 61:1 notes that "He has sent me to bind up the brokenhearted, to proclaim freedom for the captives and release from darkness for the prisoners" (NIV). Psalm 146:7 declares that "The Lord sets prisoners free" (TNIV) and Psalm 102:19-20 extols: "The Lord looked down from his sanctuary on high ... to hear the groans of the prisoners and release those condemned to death" (TNIV).

ACTIVATE
Offer to donate skills to an anti-torture or social justice ministry.

Some have read these passages as a metaphor for the Lord setting free those imprisoned by sin and releasing those condemned to death by sin. But given God's indisputable passion for justice, surely the literal meaning of these verses must also be true—that God really does seek to bring physical rescue and renewal to those dying in jail cells for crimes they did not commit, those who have had their freedom and dignity arbitrarily stripped away by more powerful enemies, and those suffering dehumanizing acts of torture at the hands of a government that should be protecting them from those very abuses.

The Lord is appalled by the suffering of injustice and is astonished when we fail to intervene. The Old Testament tells us that "the Lord looked and was displeased that there was no justice. He saw that there was no one, he was appalled that there was no one to intervene" (Isa. 59:15-16, TNIV).

> "But God will never forget the needy; the hope of the afflicted will never perish."
> —PSALM 9:18, TNIV

I suppose God's astonishment is not surprising. We often talk about injustice, but do so very little. We said "never again" after the Holocaust but turned our backs on Rwanda while more than 800,000 people lost their lives by the edge of a machete and the blunt surface of a club. Despite God's heart for the oppressed, the history of Christianity is littered with instances in which God's people failed to do the right thing at the right time.

Imagine it. Human inaction—our failure to intercede in the face of global injustices like torture and abusive detention—astonishes the Maker of the universe. But God does something truly amazing with these stories of suffering and abuse. Just as He took on our sin on the cross, He takes on the suffering of those who languish in prisons. Their story becomes God's story. Jesus says in Matthew 25:

> "For I was hungry and you gave me nothing to eat, I was thirsty and you gave me nothing to drink, I was a stranger and you did not invite me in, I needed clothes and you

did not clothe me, I was sick and in prison and you did
not look after me." They also will answer, "Lord, when
did we see you hungry or thirsty or a stranger or needing
clothes or sick or in prison, and did not help you?" He
will reply, "I tell you the truth, whatever you did not
do for one of the least of these, you did not do for me."
(Matt. 25:42–45, NIV)

God hates the injustice of torture and abusive detention and
wants to right it. He has a plan to do so, and that plan is us. Just as
He takes on the story of the suffering individual as His own story,
God asks us to do the same. Hebrews 13:3 calls upon each of us to
"Remember those in prison as if you were their fellow prisoners,
and those who are mistreated as if you yourselves were suffering"
(NIV). This is God's recognition that we live "in an inescapable
network of mutuality, tied in a single garment of destiny," as King
wrote in his "Letter from Birmingham Jail."

We know, then, that God has called each of us to action on
the issues of abusive detention and torture. Their suffering is our
suffering. But what needs to be done?

DOING WHAT'S RIGHT

The prohibitions on torture and abusive detention have been
disseminated wholesale around the globe. They are contained in
international conventions and national laws. But these protections
often don't reach the very individuals most susceptible to the
abuses. The protections against torture that have been sold
wholesale globally must be broadcast into the lives of the most
susceptible members of society. The poor, the sick, the widows,

and the orphans—the right to be free means nothing if it does not apply to those most vulnerable to abuse.

Why is it so hard for us to do the right thing when it comes to global injustice, specifically torture and abusive detention? I think there are three reasons. First, we are simply oblivious to the fact that we aren't doing anything. We either genuinely think we are doing all we can, or we purposefully ignore the problem because it's too painful to face.

Second, it's hard to do the right thing because the injustice seems so far away. The Bible tells us to love our neighbor, and I think if it were indeed the family next door that was being abusively detained or viciously tortured, we would do the right thing, right now—we would beg anybody with ears to give resources, contact representatives, stop the madness against our neighbors. But overseas? Africa? Asia? We can't relate. They aren't like us. At best, we feel highly detached from the suffering, separated by a geographic and cultural gulf, and at worst, we've just come to expect conflict and suffering in the world.

As distant as it may seem, the battle against torture is being fought in our own backyards, within our own government, within our own faith communities. It is not a distant battle, and we must be prepared to clothe ourselves for the fight.

Finally, I think it's difficult for us to do the right thing because we simply don't know what the right thing is. In the face of massive suffering outside of our immediate sphere of influence, we become like deer in headlights. We are bewildered by the bright light of injustice bearing down on us and have no idea which direction to move. So we stand still. What more can we possibly do?

We cannot underestimate the power of advocacy to change the world. The very center of that power lies in sharing and embracing the individual story of suffering. This story of suffering is one that God Himself has taken on and calls us to take on as our own.

I work for an organization called the International Justice Mission. IJM is a Christian human rights agency, composed of lawyers and other professionals, that takes individual cases of human rights abuse overseas and brings relief to victims and accountability to perpetrators. My colleagues and I have seen the awesome power of justice in the lives of real people who have been victims of torture, giving a face to the statistics. Tell someone that on this very day up to 80 percent of detainees in African jail cells are being held without legal cause, and you might get a slight raising of eyebrows; tell them John's story, a young man who was arrested by police and savagely beaten with a wooden stick in jail after his wife failed to respond to the sexual advances of an officer—the same officer who later served as the prosecutor in a trial on trumped-up charges against John—and you'll have before you a man or woman ready for battle.

Remember David? He had lost his arm after being shot by police and was facing a death sentence on charges of robbery because he couldn't pay a bribe. IJM took David's case, and after four months of legal

PRAY
Lord, times of desperation can bring about criminal and even diabolical behavior in Your children, causing them in turn to deeply hurt others. We know that no culture is free from torture, and we pray that those who imprison others, whether justly or unjustly, will treat their prisoners humanely and with dignity, even if those they imprison are the darkest-hearted criminals. For we know that all human beings were created in Your image and likeness and that even the darkest-hearted are capable of being transformed by Your grace. Amen.

wrangling, he was released from jail. Soon after, the five police officers involved in David's abuse were also arrested. Today, David has a love for life that is nothing short of infectious. He is currently enrolled in law school and wants to help others in need of rescue just as he was assisted in his time of greatest need.

Adriana's story was just one of numerous tales of police abusing street children in Bolivia. In response, IJM worked with Bolivian officials to train more than 2,600 police officers on proper methods of dealing with street children, the legal duties of officers vis-á-vis the children, and penalties for noncompliance with the law. At the conclusion of the training course, the officers signed a declaration agreeing to uphold the law and protect the children, signifying an understanding that they could face civil, criminal, or administrative liabilities if they fail to do so.

And Samuel? When IJM heard about Samuel languishing in a jail cell, we took his case and brought it before an African court of law. Faced with undeniable evidence of innocence and pressure from government officials, the court released Samuel from his torturous cell after four years. Samuel is a free man today, studying for his degree and caring for his family.

CHANGING THE WORLD

The cynical world tries desperately to convince us that the world of injustice cannot be changed—but the cynical world is wrong. The world does change, and history proves it. Apartheid ended in South Africa. Slavery and state-sponsored racism were extinguished in the United States. The Iron Curtain fell. The world has changed in amazing ways, and not one transpired by random happenstance. Men and women of vision, faith, and integrity made conscious decisions to ignore the naysayers and embrace the risks of change.

I believe that good people often do nothing because they cannot do everything. Because we are led to believe that our contribution is insignificant, we fail to contribute at all. But changing the world does not require that you possess the power to halt global injustice at the snap of fingers. Lao Tzu, philosopher and founder of Taoism, said that "a journey of a thousand miles begins with a single step." For IJM, the journey of changing the world starts with changing the life of one individual in the world, because the world of each oppressed or abused individual desperately needs to be changed.

And for each of us, changing the world can mean writing letters to representatives in Congress or giving time or money to organizations doing work to combat torture, abusive detention, or any other violation of human dignity. It could mean praying unceasingly. It could mean educating yourself, perhaps going into a profession that serves the suffering. Ultimately, the best tool of change we each possess is the power of our advocacy. By telling the stories of people like David, Adriana, and John, we can change the world. The true power to suffocate injustice lies in the individual story. The world of one friend who has never heard the truth is changed the instant you share a story with him or her. And through this individual change—microscopic change—comes structural change—macroscopic change. In changing one person, you automatically equip yet another to go out and change worlds as well. From one contact with one individual, each of us can set into motion a domino effect that, through the wonders of exponential growth, can literally change the world.

REAGAN DEMAS currently directs International Justice Mission's operations in Africa, developing casework strategies and advocating with local and national authorities. He also partners with U.S. government officials and an assortment of non-governmental organizations to further the human-rights work of IJM in Africa.

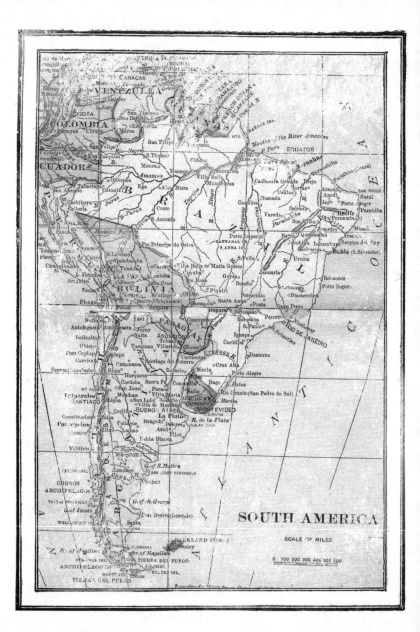

SOUTH AMERICA

SCALE OF MILES

0 100 200 300 400 500 600

THE
ENVIRONMENT

BY PETER ILLYN

"MAN HAS BEEN ENDOWED WITH REASON,
WITH THE POWER TO CREATE, SO THAT HE
CAN ADD TO WHAT HE'S BEEN GIVEN. BUT UP
TO NOW HE HASN'T BEEN A CREATOR, ONLY A
DESTROYER. FORESTS KEEP DISAPPEARING,
RIVERS DRY UP, WILDLIFE'S BECOME EXTINCT,
THE CLIMATE'S RUINED AND THE LAND GROWS
POORER AND UGLIER EVERY DAY."
—ANTON CHEKHOV

In October of 2005, anti-poverty organization World Bank revealed that nearly one-fifth of all ill health and millions of deaths in poor countries can be attributed to environmental factors like climate change and pollution. World Bank's report cited things like unsafe water, poor sanitation and hygiene, indoor and outdoor air pollution, soil pollution, pesticides, hazardous waste and chemicals in food as contributing to illness, death, and delayed economic development. Climate change due to environmental destruction has even caused a rise in the spread of diseases like malaria and dengue fever and has contributed to lower accumulation of free salts in the soil, leading to soil and vegetation degradation.

The report also linked different types of cancer to environmental conditions, saying that global warming has a major impact on health.[1]

DONATE
Learn about the various environmental advocacy groups and organizations, and make a donation to one.

As bleak as this information sounds, the report revealed that for almost all forms of cancer, risk can be reduced if physical environments are safe for human habitation and food items are safe for consumption.

I find this report disturbing. As a Christian environmental evangelist, I spend my days working to help Christians reconnect to the biblical call to love, serve, and protect God's creation. Sadly, what I find is that most evangelical Christians have little concern for the earth or, even worse, are actually hostile to environmental concerns. I am baffled by this disconnect. It defies logic and common sense.

Let's face a simple fact: there is no other planet in the known universe that can support life. Not one flower or leaf. Not one microbe. Not one strand of DNA can be found anywhere. Nothing. Nada. This fact is irrefutable, and the implications of ignoring it have profoundly disturbing results.

Yet ignore we do. Our modern culture is rooted in the myth that humans are not governed by the laws of nature—we believe we can disrespect the web of life at no cost to ourselves.

This myth is perpetuated by the illogical rhetoric of what I call "Utilitarian Christians." Their worldview is rooted in the false choice of "man versus nature"—the belief that God made the earth with little intrinsic value outside of its function in the free-market economy.

Sadly, the thinking of modern humanity has been reduced to this false dichotomy, one that ignores the inextricable fact that we are utterly dependent on the natural world for the very breath of life.

The conundrum is that humans have been given both a power over nature and a responsibility for nature. We have the technology to destroy that which we need to survive. We are connected to and dependent upon nature for our life. This is proven over and over again by science, logic, and history, yet ignored by much of Western Christianity.

Instead, what is offered as modern wisdom is the concept that we are free to do what we please to the earth—that every person has a God-given right to make as much money as he can as fast and as often as he can, all consequences be damned. The unrestrained pursuit of profits is seen as God's divine plan for humanity. And those who try to slow them down are attacked as new-world-order socialists or earth-worshipping alarmists.

I travel to a lot of developing countries, and I always enjoy returning home to appreciate the fruits of capitalism. As caretakers of God's earth, we have the right to take fruit from the garden. That is our privilege. But we do not have the right to destroy the fruitfulness thereof. Our stewardship must be measured by other-mindedness, interconnectedness, and sustainability. Jesus illustrates this principle when He asked the disciples, "Who then is the faithful and wise servant, whom the master has put in charge of the servants in his household to give them their food at the proper time?" (Matt. 24:45, TNIV).

That's my core message: the premise of environmental justice is that the stability of human life is dependent on the fruitfulness of the web of life that is itself dependent on the dynamic yet balanced cycles of nature. All creation, therefore, is interconnected and interdependent. If you disrupt this natural balance of the earth's systems, you ultimately disrupt the very survival of human life. And sadly, the first to suffer will be the poor and the sick.

THE SCIENTIFIC AGE AND ENVIRONMENTAL DISREGARD

Only five hundred years ago, the best thinkers of the newly emerging scientific age still thought the earth was flat. This significant error had tragic environmental consequences. A flat earth could be endless. It could theoretically extend forever. The earth was proven round, but this new awareness coincided with the birth of colonialism and nationalism, the merchant class and the consumer class. Nations alleged that the natural resources of the newly discovered lands were gifts to them from God, blessings of riches, rewards of Christendom. National arrogance was codified as doctrines like Manifest Destiny and *terra nullius*. Indigenous people were wiped out, lands were taken, and personal fortunes made.

Though the earth was no longer seen as flat, it was still considered a big, big world. Even a mere two hundred years ago, Americans celebrated the discoveries of Lewis and Clark, who described a landscape soon to be filled by streams of covered wagons. My home in Portland, Oregon, is now home to more than one million people. Even during my father's generation there were still unexplored places. The people in the Highlands of Papua New Guinea, with whom I now work, didn't make "first contact" with the modern world until the 1940s, when soldiers stumbled into their villages during World War II.

But all changed with the birth of NASA and the synergy of space exploration with the first television generation. I have dim memories of being ten years old, sitting in front of a black-and-white television in my flannel pajamas, watching the first man walk on the moon. When the cameras looked back at the blue marble of our planet, my generation experienced the same irrefutable reality—that the earth is a finite system. I could have compared the

"If you think you are too small to be effective, you have never been in bed with a mosquito."
—BETTY REESE

television picture with the globe by my desk at school. There were no new islands to discover, no new continents to claim as our own. We had found it all.

The space age also brought satellites that were able to track the cycles of nature and computers that could analyze the data. We could now track ocean currents, hurricanes, and weather patterns and measure the increasing level of air pollution. We could see polluted rivers bursting into flames.

THE BIRTH OF THE ENVIRONMENTAL MOVEMENT

In 1970, one year after the first man walked on the moon, America responded by hosting the first Earth Day, and the modern environmental movement was born. Now, three decades later, environmental concerns are ignored and attacked by many, including some who proclaim to be Christians. And yet, I have great hope because I'm seeing a generation living a faith that honors the world's people and our earth. There is a growing awareness that "life is sacred."

I am not sure why there is a passion for justice and community rising from the eighteen-to-thirty-five-year-old demographic within Christendom. Maybe it's the outcome of countless church missions trips to developing nations or simply the result of being raised with cable television and the Internet, but there is an expanded sense of community and stewardship of God's creation.

Environmental justice recognizes that everything in life is connected, that the web of life is just that—a web, and that all the strands must work together to ensure integrity and strength. Environmental justice recognizes that humanity is not separate from the natural world—we are a *part* of the natural world; we *are* nature. When the balance of nature is unraveled, chaos and tragedy follow. When we hurt the earth, we hurt the poor. When we hurt the earth, we hurt ourselves.

THE IMPACT OF HUMANKIND

Instead of acknowledging this simple truth, today's dominant Christian culture in America has treated ecological sustainability and environmental justice as irrelevant concerns—the ignorable rants of pagans, radicals, and tree huggers. We've been seduced into thinking that humans are no longer governed by the laws of nature, that somehow we are immune to any negative consequences resulting from the mistreatment of the earth and the unraveling of its systems.

How did this happen? How does a culture create an economy that falls prey to such a belief? Sadly, it is easy to do.

It is pure disconnect. Disconnect from cause and effect, from the consequences, from the responsibility, from the future.

In the days following Hurricane Katrina, we were reminded that human life is completely connected to the balance of nature. Our televisions brought a cultural awakening, and while watching havoc and violence erupt in New Orleans, we realized this relationship is remarkably frail and vulnerable. All hell broke loose when thousands of people realized how easily they can die.

Christianity teaches that humans are unique in all of God's creation—only we are made in the image of God, and we alone have the divinely given capacity of self-awareness and free will. We alone create art and music, build tools, and construct language. Humanity has an exceptional place in the created order, but we have forgotten that we were created last and designed by God not to be independent of the rest of creation. We were made from the dust of the earth, and we will return to the earth. "But ask the animals, and they will teach you, or the birds of the air, and they will tell you; or speak to the earth, and it will teach you, or let the fish of the sea inform you. Which of all these does not know that the hand of the Lord has done this? In his hand is the life of every creature and the breath of all mankind" (Job 12:7-10, NIV).

EDUCATE
Read up on the environment and make appropriate changes in your lifestyle so you can be a better steward. Tell your friends about ways they can be better stewards of the environment and save money by adopting some simple changes in their daily lives.

All human activity has impact—from cooking yams over an open fire in a tropical rain forest to hunting caribou for winter meat to developing another nameless megamall in another nameless city. This is not necessarily bad. This is part of dominion—the biblical call to rule and subdue, to tend to and keep creation. But I want to make a plea for the prayerful consideration of the intrinsic fruitfulness and inherent rights of all of God's creation: the entire thing, not just the human portion of it, has value—the entire miraculous, interconnected, awe-inspiring, interdependent web of life.

The moral dilemma occurs when our behaviors are unsustainable and the ecological consequences irreversible. When we drive species to extinction, lay waste to ecosystems, or exploit and destroy indigenous cultures, then our behaviors are unjust, and we risk divine judgment. Revelation 11:18 says, "The time has come for judging the dead, and for rewarding your servants the prophets and your people who revere your name, both great and small—and for destroying those who destroy the earth" (TNIV). Simply put, destroying the earth dishonors the name of God.

THE THREAT OF GLOBAL WARMING

One of the most critical issues of environmental justice is the debate over global warming. The evidence of human-caused climate change is overwhelming, but as a nation we have refused to seriously engage in policies to help prevent global warming and to stem resultant environmental destruction. For many in our culture, profiteering becomes the highest and greatest use of God's creation. Wealth is God's reward for our faithfulness. We elevate individualism and consumerism above all else.

This has happened at the highest levels of government. At a press conference concerning the U.S. energy policy, President Bush's press secretary, Ari Fleischer, was asked by a reporter, "Does the president believe that, given the amount of energy Americans consume per capita, how much it exceeds any other citizen in any other country in the world, does the president believe we need to correct our lifestyles to address the energy problem?" Fleischer responded, "That's a big 'no.' The president believes that it's an American way of life and that it should be the goal of policy makers to protect the American way of life ... The American way of life is a blessed one. The place that the American people get most of their energy that we are dependent on to preserve the American way of life does come from fossil fuels."[2]

Global warming—and its predominate cause, the rate at which humanity is burning fossil fuels—is making us look anew at how the world works. It asks fundamental questions about whether, and how, we will achieve human development, about how the global economy can run within the environmental limits of the planet's life-support system, and about the obligation of the wealthy to aid the impoverished.

> "Then God said, 'Let us make man in our image, in our likeness, and let them rule over the fish of the sea and the birds of the air, over the livestock, over all the earth, and over all the creatures that move along the ground.'"
>
> —GENESIS 1:26, NIV

Global warming results in more extreme weather patterns, more rain, longer dry spells, stronger and more violent storms, more fires, and the spread of tropical diseases. Ironically, while the developed nations of the world produce the majority of the greenhouse gases, the burden of the impact will be more severe on developing countries whose populations are poorer and thereby more vulnerable and less equipped to deal with the extreme events of droughts, floods, and hurricanes.

These present the most direct risks to the poor. In coastal areas, heavier rains caused by rising sea levels will increasingly cause flooding and landslides. With sea levels set to rise by more than three feet in the coming century, heavily populated areas of low-lying land face a bleak future.

FIGHTING FOR THE EARTH

But statistics, dire warnings, and a call to duty do not seem to be enough of a motivator for our culture to change behavior. I believe the first step in environmental justice is to reconnect to the miracle of life. We have to return from seeing the earth strictly as a commodity to seeing it as an integral part of our human community.

Was the reckless disrespect for our planet in the heart of Adam when he named the animals? Can you hear it in this cry of the Alaskan native?

> We told these [visitors] we liked the mountains and we liked the sea. We liked to spend as much time in these places as we could, the frozen sea, the snowy mountains, the summer sea, this gorgeous, ever changing, breathtaking country which is our homeland. Nowhere else is all of this possible, a sea full of great whales and seals and fish and polar bear and foxes and birds of every kind, from nearly every land, with mountains just nearby full of white sheep and wolves and wolverine and with great plain in between the mountains and the sea with muskoxen and caribou and river and lake fish and many more birds and a thousand other things, all intermingled with the spirits and memories and stories and legends and frames and old

houses of our people. This is the perfect place, the perfect place for us, which is why God probably put us here, these few of us, and made us tough enough to stay.[3]

My ministry, Restoring Eden, frequently works with tribal Christians. I see injustice most clearly when I try to look at the modern world through their eyes. For example, when I was traveling around Papua New Guinea speaking to tribal church leaders, I met Yat Paol, the son of a tribal chief and a committed Christian.

I've been privileged to spend a lot of time with Yat Paol, traveling in a four-wheel truck from tribe to tribe in the jungles of Papua New Guinea and driving a van and pulling a giant slab of an ancient Douglas fir tree in America, a stump that was 450 years old. Yat and I would park on a college campus and, using the stump as a sermon illustration, discuss the history of Christianity in America and the legacy of environmental destruction that soon followed.

Many times, to save money, we would sleep in the van, talking late into the night about his culture, about the world before "first contact," before his people knew there was a modern world.

I remember one conversation well, a

ACTIVATE

• Participate in local environmental action groups, both political and other (i.e., litter cleanup, gardening organizations).

• Consider reducing or altogether eliminating meat and other animal products from your diet.

• Buy locally grown and organic produce.

• Drive a fuel-efficient car.

• Reduce, reuse, and recycle.

• Take measures to ensure that your home is as energy efficient as possible.

• Lobby your local and state representatives to take action on important environmental issues.

PRAY

Lord, You created us to be stewards of Your creation. Please help us to recognize the earth You have given us as our home as a precious resource filled with delightful gifts to be harvested carefully, rather than recklessly exploited. Grant us the foresight to live simply and use the earth's resources conservatively, and help us to always remember Your goodness in each breath of clean, life-sustaining air we inhale, thanking You and always being awestruck by the unmatched splendor of Your creation. Amen.

moment where my understanding was expanded. "You should have warned us about greed," Yat told me. "We had no word for it. In our world nothing of value could be hoarded—all wealth was all biodegradable. To take more than you needed was self-defeating. If you caught more fish than you could use today, then tomorrow all you had was a pile of rotting fish and risked no fish in the future. We took only what we needed and shared everything we had. Our lives depended upon it. We never knew we were poor until you taught us about money."

Yat told me that back at their remote coastal village they call themselves "bellybutton Christians" because they still consider their umbilical cord connected to their mother, the earth. She gives them shelter, food, medicine, and even embraces their dead in her arms. Yat went on to say that when tribal members move into the cities, back at the village they say that they have "lost their bellybuttons"—their life-giving connection to their mother.

I was also privileged to travel to Christian colleges with a Gwich'in minister, the Reverend Trimble Gilbert, who was the village priest and the traditional elder of the caribou people of northern Alaska.

My vision is to fight "development." I want my people to stay healthy, to have clean water, to be able to continue with subsistence fishing and hunting. I want them to keep our language. I want us to retain our beliefs and identity as Athabascans, our values of sharing and respect. As the scripture says, honor your father and mother so that you will have a long life. The Gwich'in way is to live as one big family, close to each other. We can't move away, because that would hurt the family. We have lived this way for thousands of years. The Gwich'in gift is to listen and learn from God. We teach one another to love, show kindness and humility, treat others with equality. We are a strong spiritual people. We know that the way God created the world is good, and we look for the renewal of the world. We can remind others what it is to have a people and a place. I even hope our whole country can be united based on these values.[4]

For tribal people around the world, human rights and environmental justice are inextricably connected. The government of Papua New Guinea, a nation formed a mere thirty years ago from a land of a thousand tribes, is being pressured by the International Money Fund to register all tribal land so it can be sold or used as collateral for foreign development projects. But for the tribes, land is traditionally held in trust by the entire tribe—tribal land cannot be sold. Land is life.

Individuals had the right to use and benefit from the land, but no right to sell it or destroy it. So when the Papua New Guinea government tried to force the people to register their land as private property, a large group of college students marched in the capital. To the student protestors, this was corrupted Western thinking being forced on them. When the peaceful protestors reached the capitol building, a large group of police confronted the students and shot four of them dead. It was Kent State all over again.

A riot erupted, with hundreds of people looting, burning, and marching down the road in front of the home where I was staying. I first heard, and then saw coming over the hill, a mix of tribal leaders, yelling, waving sticks, and shaking palm leaves as they descended toward the government headquarters. Marching with the students were Papua New Guinea soldiers, armed with assault rifles and bullets, ready to confront the offending policemen. Fortunately, there were no more deaths.

Later that day, Yat and I met with the U.S. ambassador. As we discussed the riots, she exclaimed, "I don't get your people. Don't they want development?" Yat, ever the diplomat, held his sometimes-caustic tongue until we got outside. Then he vented. "I don't get her people. Doesn't she realize that for us, land is life? We are not protesting development, we are protecting our mother. It is inconceivable to sell your mother!"

This connection to the earth is endemic to every indigenous culture. I also learned this from Trimble Gilbert, the Gwich'in tribal leader and Episcopal priest who said the legends of his people teach that every caribou has a bit of the human heart in him, and every human has a bit of caribou heart.

> It's part of the Gwich'in connection to the land. The caribou are our main source of food. When we have to be away in the city, our spirit becomes weak. We need caribou meat, we need fish. We need to be in our land. Farther south in Fort Yukon, people catch salmon and

beaver, and in other areas the main animal is moose. We sometimes trade caribou for these other meats. Sometimes we have suffered famines, with no caribou for several years. Then our people had to move to Fort Yukon, where residents shared their food with us. The same happens when they run low on food; we help each other.[5]

WHAT YOU CAN DO

Better stewardship of the earth begins with a shift in perspective and a few small steps. Fall back in love with nature. Become like a six-year-old at the zoo. Rediscover the intrinsic goodness of creation. Understand the interconnectedness of the web of life. Worship the Creator with the great choir of creation. Love, serve, and protect God's creation. Become a grassroots activist. Work to build political will for policies that are other-minded, long-sighted, and tender-hearted. Measure your ecological footprint. Inventory your lifestyle. Identify ways that you can cut back and live more simply. If everyone were to make an effort to conserve the earth's invaluable energy and resources, the positive impact on our environment would be great.

PETER ILLYN spent years as an evangelical minister until a one-thousand-mile llama trek through the Cascade wilderness turned him into an unabashed environmental activist. He is the founder of Restoring Eden, a ministry dedicated to helping the Church rediscover the biblical calling to love, serve, and protect God's creation as advocates of native species, wild habitats, and indigenous cultures.

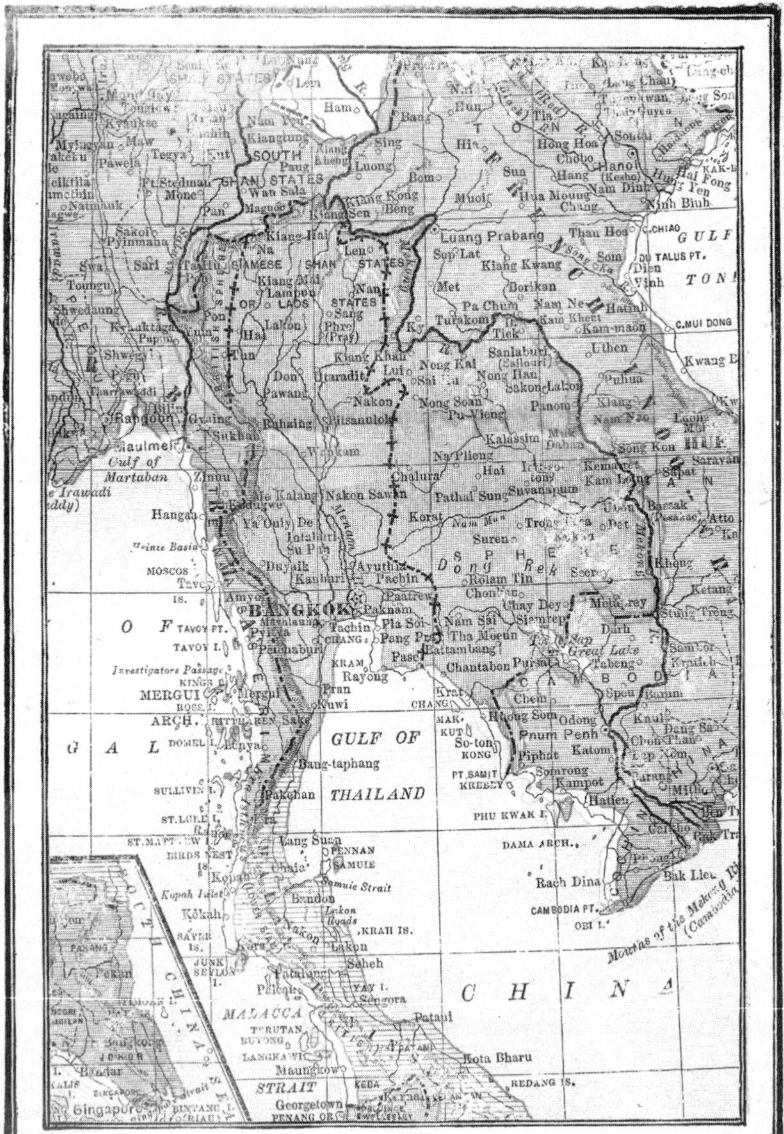
SHAN STATES
Lem
Ham
Nam Yeu
Kiangtung
SOUTH
SHAN STATES
Wan Sala
Pan
Mone
Kyaukse
Pawela
Tegya
Sing
Luong
Bom
Kiang Kong
Beng
Kiang Sen
Luang Prabang
Sop Lat
Kiang Kwang
Met
Borikan
Pa Chum
Nam Neu
Turakom
Hua Moung
Chang
Thau Hoa
Hong Hoa
Chobo
Hanoi
Hang
Nam Dinh
Hai Fong
Hung Yen
Ninh Binh
Sontai
GULF
TONK
C. MUI DONG
DU TALUS PT.
Dien
Vinh
Hatinh
Kam-maon
Uthen
Kwang B
Kiang Hai
SIAMESE
SHAN
STATES
Nan
STATES
Kiang Mai
Lampun
OR
LAOS
Sang
Phre
(Praf)
Lakon
Tun
Pon
Sakoi
Pyinmana
Sari
Swa
Toungu
Shwedaung
Papun
Shwegyi
Pegu
Tharrawaddi
Rangoon
Maulmein
Gulf of
Martaban
Irawadi
Hangaa
Zimmu
Sukhai
Kiang Khan
Lui
Utaradit
Nong Kai
Nong Han
Sakon
Lakon
Sanlaburi
(Sallouri)
Panom
Puhua
Nakon
Don
Pawang
Buhaing
Pitsanulok
Nong Soan
Pu-Vieng
Kalassim
Na Plieng
Hai
Kemarat
Kam Long
Song Kon
Sarayan
Chalura
Nakon Sawan
Me Kalang
Pathai Sung
Suvanapun
Korat
Mun
Surena
Bassak
(Passac)
Atto
Khong
Dong Rek
Ayuthia
Pachin
Kanburi
Rolam Tin
Sserey
Ketang
Stung Treng
MOSCOS
Tavoy
IS.
Amyo
BANGKOK
Paknam
Paatrew
Chay Dey
Siamrep
Moulpey
Durh
OF
TAVOY PT.
TAVOY I.
Tachin
Pla Soi
Pang Pra
Nam Sai
Tha Moeun
Battambang
Pasel
Chantabon
Pursat
Great Lake
Tabeng
CAMBODIA
Kratieh
Sambor
Investigators Passage
MERGUI
KINGS I.
Mergui
ROSS I.
ARCH.
KRAM
Rayong
Pran
Kuwi
CHANG
Krat
Chem
Spen
Banam
Huong Som
Odong
Pnum Penh
Kaul
Dang Sa
MAK.
KUT
So-ton
KONG
Piphat
Katom
Chon Than
GAL
DOMEL I.
Lenya
GULF OF
THAILAND
Bang-taphang
PT. SAMIT
KREBEY
Somrong
Kampot
Hatien
Mitho
SULLIVIN I.
Pakchan
ST. LUKE I.
PHU KWAK I.
Canthe
Lang Suan
PENNAN
SAMUIE
DAMA ARCH.
ST. MATTHEW I.
BIRDS NEST IS.
Kopah
Chaia
Samuie Strait
Kopah Inlet
Bandon
Lakon
Roads
Rach Dina
Bak Lieu
CAMBODIA PT.
OBI I.
Mouths of the Mekong R.
(Cambodia
Kokah
SAYER IS.
KRAH IS.
Lakon
JUNK
SEYLON I.
Patalang
Soheh
YAY I.
Sengora
CHINA
MALACCA
Patani
TRUTAN
BUTONG
LANGKAWI
Maungkow
Kota Bharu
STRAIT
KEDA
REDANG IS.
Georgetown
PENANG
SOUTH CHINA SEA
PAHANG
Pekan
JOHOR
Bandar
SINGAPORE
Singapore
BINTANG I.
(RIAU)

CHAPTER ELEVEN

HUMAN TRAFFICKING

BY PENNY HUNTER

"THIS IS THE DUTY OF OUR GENERATION
AS WE ENTER THE TWENTY-FIRST
CENTURY—SOLIDARITY WITH THE WEAK, THE
PERSECUTED, THE LONELY, THE SICK, AND
THOSE IN DESPAIR. IT IS EXPRESSED BY THE
DESIRE TO GIVE A NOBLE AND HUMANIZING
MEANING TO A COMMUNITY IN WHICH ALL
MEMBERS WILL DEFINE THEMSELVES NOT
BY THEIR OWN IDENTITY BUT BY THAT OF
OTHERS." —ELIE WIESEL

A Google search of "natural disasters" yields dozens of events we've witnessed in our lifetime. Surely any twenty- or thirtysomething could recap the devastation of the Indonesian tsunami of 2004 or Hurricane Katrina in 2005. These disasters have been catastrophic, and thousands have lost their lives. But beyond the front pages of our newspapers, there's a hidden, man-made disaster occurring day in and day out that should not escape our notice. It is the epidemic of human trafficking.

This disaster affects millions of people, and it is preventable. Trafficking in persons only flourishes where there is a market demand by humans for humans and where local law enforcement tolerates the practice. Therefore, we have it in our power to abolish this hideous slavery by holding our brothers and sisters accountable for the sale of other human beings. Around the world, there are criminal laws that prohibit slavery and provide adequate protection for the victim; yet too often, the laws are not enforced, perpetrators are not held accountable, and victims go unnoticed.

DONATE
Make a donation to an anti-trafficking organization to help fund a rescue of a victim of trafficking.

Organizations such as International Justice Mission (IJM) have taken a stand against modern-day slavery by documenting cases, rescuing victims, and formally prosecuting slaveholders in violation of these laws. For most Americans, "slavery" is a word associated with the past, but it is important to realize that human trafficking, including bonded labor and sex trafficking, are today's descendent of the historical slave trade. We need modern-day abolitionists to stand shoulder to shoulder and put an end to this despicable practice.

THE FACTS ABOUT HUMAN TRAFFICKING

There is perhaps no more insidious place to find trafficking in humans than in the dirty and dingy backrooms of the world where children and women are held as sex slaves. According to the U.S. Department of State, of the 600,000 to 800,000 people trafficked across international borders every year, 80 percent are female and 70 percent are trafficked for sexual exploitation. Bluntly put, this is the business of rape for profit. Here's what this looks like: trafficked girls and women are often tricked into leaving their homes with

the promise of a good job, while others may be drugged or kidnapped. In some instances, victims are sold by family members to serve as sex slaves to pay for family medical bills or debts.

While you may find that hard to believe, there are hundreds of thousands of girls like the one IJM investigators came to know as Dacie. A woman in Dacie's village invited the teenager to go to the city over her school break with the promise of earning a little extra money working in a noodle shop. This job would provide for some relief for her family as they struggled to make ends meet.

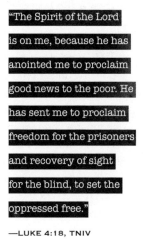

"The Spirit of the Lord is on me, because he has anointed me to proclaim good news to the poor. He has sent me to proclaim freedom for the prisoners and recovery of sight for the blind, to set the oppressed free."

—LUKE 4:18, TNIV

The trusted woman from her village was actually a player in the game of trafficking. After Dacie had been transported to the city, she was told that she would not be selling noodles, but instead would be forced to submit her body to frequent and brutal rape by men who paid brothel keepers to have sex with her. When Dacie vocally objected and cried out during the rape by her first customer, who paid a premium to violate a virgin, the brothel keeper came into the room and wrapped Dacie's mouth with duct tape to silence her protests. Alone, facing a hopeless situation far from her family, Dacie was subjected to constant abuse.

IJM investigators infiltrated the brothel where Dacie was kept and worked with local police to organize a raid. Dacie was among the girls ultimately freed by the police and was placed in a loving aftercare home where she received counsel until she was reunited with her family. Amazingly, at the time of Dacie's rescue, her sister was also being held at the brothel while waiting for her first customer. She had become ensnared in the same web as Dacie. Thankfully, though, Dacie's sister was rescued before she was raped.

IJM investigators have learned of hundreds of girls like Dacie. Upon arriving at brothels, these victims are forced to have unprotected sex numerous times a day in deplorable conditions where disease is rampant. UNICEF estimates that approximately one million children are forced into the commercial sex industry every year and are the most vulnerable to contracting and spreading HIV/AIDS. For these victims, there is no such thing as "safe sex" or the freedom to choose sexual partners. They are forcibly infected with HIV/AIDS and suffer the dehumanizing battering of their self-worth. The heartbreaking reality is that for girls not rescued, time is ticking quickly as brothel keepers and sex tourists barter over the bodies of these youngsters.

THE DILEMMA OF PUTTING AN END TO TRAFFICKING

Many ask why something isn't being done if the problem is solvable. As IJM investigators can attest, it is not hard to find trafficking victims. Men seeking sex with young children and women can easily find them for sale. Low-level police corruption and organized crime fuel trafficking, as they receive a cut of the revenue through bribes paid by pimps or brothel keepers. The temptation for police officers to accept bribes in exchange for overlooking or aiding the problem of trafficking is especially great because of the low wages they commonly receive, making them financially vulnerable and thus susceptible to the exploitation of traffickers. Fairly compensated, better-trained police officers could be a vital resource in the fight against trafficking, rather than a part of the problem. The FBI estimates that worldwide, human trafficking generates about $9.5 billion annually.

EDUCATE
Watch the film *Born into Brothels* and learn about the impact of trafficking on people's lives. Spread the word.

How can we stop these crimes against humanity? We can increase U.S. public awareness on current laws such as the Protect Act, which allows for the prosecution of Americans who travel overseas for sex with trafficking victims, and continued congressional enforcement of the annual Trafficking in Persons (TIP) Report, distributed by the State Department. The TIP Report ranks the world's countries on a three-tier level based on each country's compliance with the minimum standards for the elimination of trafficking set forth in the 2000 Trafficking Victims Protection Act.

The solution to trafficking lies in a concerted, determined effort to bring relief to victims and accountability to perpetrators. IJM investigators have spent thousands of hours infiltrating brothels, documenting victims, and presenting evidence to secure police contacts to provide for the rescue of these victims who would otherwise languish as sex slaves. Through structural change, increased awareness, rescue, and accountability, we may someday see the abolition of the trade of humans.

We also must confront the fact that the vast majority of these victims live in far corners of the world—thousands of miles away from our cul-de-sacs, ivy-walled college campuses, and climate-controlled shopping malls. These women and girls may not look like our next-door neighbors. They may speak a different language, have a different skin color, and celebrate a culture foreign to ours. It's easy to dismiss problems that are not in our face day after day. It's easy to view trafficking as someone else's problem.

THE CALL TO CARE

As friends of Jesus, however, we cannot so easily dismiss our role. In the Gospels, Jesus often turns our thinking on its ear because of the way He describes how large our circle of compassion should be. In Luke 10, Jesus takes a moment to tell an important story that most elementary students could grasp. He asked the simple question, "Who is our neighbor?" The simply and undeniable answer is anyone in need. Gary Haugen, founder of IJM, challenged me with his response to the tsunami devastation. Though orphaned children were at risk of trafficking, it wasn't until a blond, blue-eyed European child disappeared that Westerners sat up and took notice. Haugen reminded us that our concern is inadequate unless we care for all of God's children: "We will not be able to combat this evil until we care as much about children who do not look like our own as we do those who do."

It is very easy to recite, "For God so loved the world," but quite another thing to actually love the world ourselves. Bulging hearts of compassion and selflessness are required to embrace God's plan to love the world through us as an extension of Him loving the world through His son. The marvelous thing about God's plan to bring rescue and hope to the oppressed is that He really doesn't need us to do it. He invites us purposefully so we might participate in the joy of laboring with Him. The joy of seeing freedom come for others. The joy of seeing our circle of compassion grow in a way that reflects His character.

"When justice is done, it brings joy to the righteous" (Prov. 21:15, TNIV).

At IJM, we believe modern-day slavery can be abolished, counting on the fact that this is God's perfect will. Justice is a theme we find throughout Scripture; God is close to the oppressed. The psalmist says, "He will rescue them from oppression and violence, for precious is their blood in his sight" (Ps. 72:14, TNIV). God is looking for women and men of faith and courage to be instruments of His mercy and justice on behalf of the oppressed.

ACTIVATE

- Donate your services to an anti-trafficking organization.

- Consider becoming an advocate for slaves. Read the article "Preparing for a Career in Human Rights" by Gary Haugen at *www.ijm.org* to learn more.

- Tell your elected officials that human trafficking is a problem that cannot be ignored and ask them to take action on the political level to stop trafficking.

WHAT YOU CAN DO

HEAR GOD'S HEART. Study passages about justice and oppression and see the priority God has placed on these topics.

PRAY FOR VICTIMS AND PERPETRATORS. As you read this, people are being bought and sold. Pray for the protection of

PRAY

Lord, we know that You once said that if anyone causes one of these little ones who believe in You to sin, it would be better for him to have a large millstone hung around his neck and to be drowned in the depths of the sea (Matt. 18:6). Humans who are bought, sold, and abused physically and sexually for the benefit of others are these precious little ones; and while we pray in earnest that You liberate those who are being unjustly sold as slaves in the darkest corners of the world, we sincerely ask that You transform the hearts of those who would so cruelly enslave other human beings, as such a sickness that drives humans to treat others as chattel is a deep, dark sickness that desperately calls out for a cure. Please help us to put aside our evil desires and love our neighbors as we love ourselves. Amen.

these victims, for justice for the slave traders, and for speedy rescue.

PAY FOR THE RESCUE THE POOR CAN'T AFFORD.

Organizations like IJM depend on gifts from individuals to allow them to bring rescue and relief.

TALK ABOUT IT. Use your influence in your circle of friends, colleagues, small groups, etc. to raise awareness for this issue. Consider doing a Bible study on the topic.

BE PREPARED TO GO. You may be uniquely called to personally go and provide advocacy and intervention for slaves. Read the article "Preparing for a Career in Human Rights" by Gary Haugen at *www.ijm.org*.

INTEGRATE JUSTICE as part of your global witness. Encourage your pastor and missions team to add justice to their global focus.

PENNY HUNTER serves as the vice president of communications for International Justice Mission. She oversees all communications efforts for IJM, including online, video, and print. She also works in the artist community to engage creative minds to pursue an expression of justice in their work and to engage the culture by using their talents. Hunter's efforts have resulted in major news coverage for IJM.

SCALE OF MILES
0 50 100 150 200
350 Miles to the Inch
T I B E T
Chargut L.
Chicul L.
Kgaring
Yatung
Brahmaputra
Mt. Everest
NEPAL
KHATMANDU
Rudokh
Demchok
Tashikang
Dankar
Abbottabad
Srinagar
Rawalpindi
Jehlam
Bhera
Sialkot
Wazirabad
Chamba
Gujranwala
Chiniot
Lahore
Sukhet
Amritsar
Simla
Jhang
Ferozpur
Ludiana
Kapurthala
Multan
Patiala
Umballah
Dehra
Dadur
Moauffernugger
Saharanpur
Panibat
Almora
Hansi
Meerut
Rampur
Khanpur
Great
Desert
Bhiwana
Delhi
Moradabad
Rohri
Bikanir
Bareilly
Khyrpur
Phatodi
Budaun
Shahjahanpur
Aligarh
Alwar
Muttra
Nagur
Jaypur
Bharatpur
Farruckabad
Jaysalmir
Oudh
Kishangarh
Ajmir
Agra
Lucknow
Gorakhpur
Jodhpur
Dholpur
Faizabad
Haidarabad
Nasirabad
Gwalior
Cawnpur
Umrkot
Jaller
Tonk
Jhansi
Futtehpur
Jaunpur
Ghazipur
Dinajpur
Darbhanga
Dalia
Allahabad
Sironi
Benares
Kotah
Nugur Parkur
Chattrpur
Rewa
Mirzapur
Disa
Nimoerah
Guna
Mundesur
Palanpur
Pattan
Shahgarh
Saipur
Palamow
Rajgarh
Dungarpur
Bhopal
Sagar
N D I A
Ahmadabad
Rutlam
Ujjain
Jabalpur
Sohagpur
Korea
Ranchi
Bardawan
Nadjad
Indur
Howrah
Rajkot
Mhow
Ramgarh
Midnapur
Burwani
Hoshangabad
Junagarh
Bharuch
Hindia
Chindwara
Ratanpur
Balasur
Ellichpur
Bhaunagar
Burhanpur
Gowilgarh
Raipur
Bombra
Bhadrak
Surat
Narnalla
Nagpur
(Nagpore)
Daman
(to Port.)
Akola
Amraoti
Patna
Gulf of Cambay
Blaisawal
Nawagarh
Bod
Kuttack
Mahanadi
Karlar
Danu
Aurangabad
Thana
Chanda
Junnaguddao
Juganath
Bombay
Ahmadnagar
Godavari
Ganjam (Puri)
Jagdalpur
Khalyan
Nander
DIRECTION BK.
Poona
Ramgarh
Jaipur
B E N G
Satara
Mullangar
Chicacole
Mahabaleshwar
Sholapur
Bidar
Golkonda
Ratnagiri
Vizagapatam
Miraj
Kulbarga
ANGRIA BANK
Vizadrug
Kolhapur
Haidarabad
Rajamahendri
Kollkonda
Belgaum
Yanaon (Fr.)
Malwan
Masulipatnam
Goa or Panjim
(to Port.)
Karnul
Dharwad
Hubli
Adoni
Ongole
Ballari
ADAS BK.
Honawar
Harihal
Nagar
Kudapa
Nellur
Kundapur
Chitaldrug
B A Y
Harihar
Reniguota
Karimar
Malabar
Bangalore
Chittur
Madras
Vellore
Mangalore
Chengalpatt
Mercara
O F
Kannanore
Mysore
Pondicheri (Fr.)
Mahe (Fr.)
Wynad
Salem
Coast
Cuddalur
Kalikut
B E N G A
Koimbatur
LAKKADIV ISLANDS
(British)
Coast
Tanjur
Karikal (Fr.)
Trichur
Trichinopoli
Nagapatnam
Madura
Palk Str.
Cochin
Ramnad
Jaffna
Nine Degree Channel
Quilon
Kokelay
Tinnevelli
Tuttukudi
Trincomali
Trivanderam
I N D I A N
Puttlam
CAPE COMORIN
CEYLON

CHAPTER TWELVE

POVERTY

BY CRANFORD JOSEPH COULTER

———————

"THE BREAD WHICH YOU DO NOT USE IS
THE BREAD OF THE HUNGRY. THE GARMENT
HANGING IN YOUR WARDROBE IS THE GARMENT
OF THE ONE WHO IS NAKED. THE SHOES THAT
YOU DO NOT WEAR ARE THE SHOES OF THE
ONE WHO IS BAREFOOT. THE MONEY YOU KEEP
LOCKED AWAY IS THE MONEY OF THE POOR.
THE ACTS OF CHARITY YOU DO NOT PERFORM
ARE SO MUCH INJUSTICES YOU COMMIT."
—SAINT BASIL THE GREAT

———————

I have grown to truly delight in daylilies. We have about a half
dozen varieties in our backyard. They are so amazing! They produce
enormous, brilliantly colored blossoms, each one a work of art
superior to any likeness that Georgia O'Keeffe or Pierre Auguste
Renoir could ever produce. Then they are gone in a day.

"Consider how the lilies grow. They do not labor or spin. Yet I tell you, not even Solomon in all his splendor was dressed like one of these" (Luke 12:27, NIV).

Anyone who walks with me into our backyard while these lilies are blooming will hear me say, "Consider today's lily!" The daylily blossom is a reminder of God's great care for us. He made them beautiful for us to enjoy. He made them wither in a day, to be replaced by another blossom as uniquely beautiful as the last, in order to illustrate His abundant provision for us. They passage goes on to instruct us as to the urgency of doing what is good today.

> If that is how God clothes the grass of the field, which is here today, and tomorrow is thrown into the fire, how much more will he clothe you, O you of little faith! And do not set your heart on what you will eat or drink; do not worry about it. For the pagan world runs after all such things, and your Father knows that you need them. But seek his kingdom, and these things will be given to you as well. Do not be afraid, little flock, for your Father has been pleased to give you the kingdom. Sell your possessions and give to the poor. Provide purses for yourselves that will not wear out, a treasure in heaven that will not be exhausted, where no thief comes near and no moth destroys. For where your treasure is, there your heart will be also. (Luke 12:28-34, NIV)

Jesus tells us that giving to the poor is a more secure investment than the stock market or an IRA. It is not an investment for your old age, but for what comes after that (or could come at any time, really). But, by the same token, God is promising that if we truly obey Him in giving by faith, we will always have what we need in this life.

The idea that giving to the poor is giving to God can be found throughout the Bible. It should be noted that nowhere does it mention giving only to those poor who are deserving or worthy, or those who are poor through no fault of their own. No. Giving is an act of mercy. What is mercy? It is when one is spared the negative consequences of one's misbehavior. The poor are not presumed to be innocent, nor are we to judge them to be guilty. When we are confronted by them, we are given an opportunity to respond as we would hope God would respond to us in our poverty. It is the tender mercies of God that lead men to repentance (Rom. 2:4). When you give money to a sinner in Jesus' name, you are making an investment for both his and your future in the kingdom of God.

POVERTY AND HOMELESSNESS

The problem of poverty and, more specifically, homelessness is embarrassing and puzzling. It started as a widespread phenomenon in American cities in the late 1970s and early 1980s. It has more recently spread to Europe. There are varying and conflicting theories as to the cause or causes of homelessness. Some blame homeless people for poor lifestyle choices. Others blame the system that has eliminated cheaper housing while not increasing minimum wage or assistance. There is truth and error in both theories, but I don't find the usual discussion particularly edifying or fruitful. The research is scant and largely flawed. We don't even have a good handle on how many homeless people there are, much less how they got there. Many homeless people will deny that they are homeless, either because of the shame that has been attached to homelessness or because they are in denial of their situation and see it as temporary. The only real cause of homelessness is sin—and there's plenty of that to go around to all concerned. Sin, according to Jesus Christ, is falling short of perfect love. To fulfill the whole Law, we need to love the Lord with all of our hearts and love our neighbors as ourselves. So whether it is the particular sin of a system that is willing to treat labor as a commodity that can be manipulated and controlled so as to make people work at low wages or the particular sin of laziness, it starts from a failure to love.

I started The King's Jubilee (TKJ) in 1989, after I was sent to assist urban churches to minister to the homeless and poor after leading inmates in Bible studies at the State Correctional Institution of Graterford, Pennsylvania. At the core of our ministry is serving a hearty meal once a week to 75 to 150 homeless people in the center of Philadelphia, on the street. We have also helped start several other ministries to the poor in seven towns and cities from Pennsylvania to South Carolina; these ministries were later adopted and continued by local churches.

DONATE
Make a donation to a national or international organization that deals with poverty, or become a regular donor to a local street ministry. Regularly go through your house and donate clothing and other things to a nonprofit thrift store.

Every human being starts his or her life with wonderful potential and hope. Each person is a unique, unrepeatable reflection of the glory of God, made in His image. This is true, whether he or she is homeless, addicted, in prison, shopping at the local grocery store, or singing next to you in choir. Each one was once a beautiful baby in someone's arms. God loves everyone we meet and sees something that is worthy of redemption. He is not willing to throw anyone away. I instruct all of the volunteers who work with TKJ to pray this simple prayer: "Lord, let me see what it is that you love about each person I meet." It is powerful. But I warn you, be prepared to have your heart broken.

STORIES FROM THE FRONTLINES

OSCAR

Let me tell you about some of my friends from the street. I will start with Oscar. I met Oscar years ago, when we were still serving at Love Park (JFK Plaza, center city Philadelphia). Oscar didn't fit the stereotypical expectations of a homeless person. He was a white guy, about forty-five years old, who enjoyed talking about philosophy, history, art, and music. He always made a point to stay and thank us for the food. He had an easygoing manner, a twinkle in his eye, and a wry wit. For a while we would see him regularly; then he would miss a couple of weeks. On one such occasion, Oscar came back and told us about how his old college friends came to town and they had a four-day party at the Four Seasons.

Once, we brought to the street several bags of clothes that missed the deadline for the truck going to Homestead, Florida, for victims of Hurricane Andrew in 1992. The people who had donated clothing tucked money into some of the pockets, knowing that the hurricane victims needed some immediate cash. I was told about this, but I had forgotten and didn't check the pockets. In one of the bags was a corduroy sport coat with suede patches on the pockets. When the guys found it, they made fun of it. Oscar grabbed it and said, "Hey, I'm not proud. It may not be stylish, but it's warm for the cool fall evenings."

Later that night he checked the pockets and found $50 cash. A couple of weeks later, he came back to tell us the story and to thank us. He said he wished that he could tell us he spent it wisely, but he had gone on a bender. I told him that I was glad he found the money. He was free to use it as he pleased. If it eased his pain for a few days, well, praise God. God commands me not to condemn Oscar, but to show mercy. Dietrich Bonhoeffer wrote: "We need to relate to people less according to what they do or omit to do, and more according to what they have suffered."

Oscar didn't make it to fifty, due to a heart weakened by cocaine use. I cannot help but remember him fondly, and I hope I see his face again one day. I was blessed by Oscar's joy and sense of humor. He was a kind and sympathetic soul.

TYRONE

Tyrone is your typical young black homeless man. I had seen him in the Philadelphia prison system before I saw him on the streets. When I met him, I said, "I'm glad to see you in the land of the living, but sorry you are in need of our service." He wanted to talk about the Lord, so we did.

This was during the time when crack and crack violence were very big on the streets. One night a fight broke out between two of the folks we served. Immediately Tyrone and a dozen others formed a human chain barricade between those of us serving and the fight. Others went in to restrain those fighting. One of the brawlers had broken a glass bottle and was trying to cut the other with it. The men around us hollered at them: "Take this away from here! This is not these people's fight."

After the fight was broken up, many of them apologized to us for it. They were amazed when we returned the next week. Tyrone asked us why we came back. I told him that God doesn't give up on me when I misbehave; He still reaches out in love to save me. The love of God is what compels me to be there. I also thanked him and the others for their bravery to stand in harm's way to protect us.

Another volunteer, Tony, spent time on various occasions talking to Tyrone about the love of God and His mercy toward us, and how it is not enough just to make a mental assent of God's love and mercy—after all, "faith without works is dead." A couple weeks later, Tyrone was

"Find out how much God has given you and from it take what you need; the remainder is needed by others."

—Saint Augustine

happy to tell us about how he had witnessed for Christ. He said that he was given some money but did not spend it all on himself, using some of it to buy condoms. He went to a block with a number of hookers on it and gave each of them some condoms, saying, "Jesus loves you. Protect yourself."

We wept tears of joy when we heard his story because we knew he had gotten it. It may not fit into any evangelism handbook, but he was doing his best to share the tender mercies of God. Consider the prostitute Rahab, whose profession of faith was expressed through her act of lying to protect the Israelite spies. The Scriptures number her among the saints (Heb. 11:31, James 2:25).

DONALD

Donald is another man God put in my life whose experience made an impact on me. He has been homeless on and off through the years. Now in his fifties, Donald was in his thirties when I met him. He would always stay after we served the food to thank us. He'd observe the crowd, which back in those days was pretty rowdy, and ask me why I put up with that and kept coming. I would tell him Jesus loved him and wouldn't let me *not* come.

Donald would say, "I don't believe in that God stuff, but you are really special people. Thank you." There were times when we wouldn't see Donald for weeks. Then he would show up again, and I would ask him where he had been. He would sometimes say that he had fallen back into cocaine use and felt ashamed to come. Jesus still loves him, I would tell him, and I missed him. He would say, "You know what I think about that God stuff, but you are something really special!"

God really put Donald on my heart. I prayed for him daily. Our exchanges continued like this for eight months. One rainy night, he said, "I thank God for you all" with a tear in his eye as he walked away.

I think I cried all the way home. Donald has been clean of cocaine ever since. He struggles. He can't find a job that pays enough to cover rent. Sometimes he goes to his parents' home, but he doesn't feel right staying there for more than a couple of months. For a while he was renting a room in the house of a man in his late eighties. He helped him out with household chores and paid him some rent. The man's daughter let him stay there for a year after the man died, until she could settle the estate and sell the house.

One night after serving, another man complained about his lot and asked how God could do this to him. Donald immediately told him to thank God for his life and for every little thing he did have. Start thanking God, he said, and things would get better. He told him, "Sure, you will still have problems, but you will be able to cope. Things will go better." Another evangelist!

NANCI

Nanci's story sheds light on the pitfalls of street ministry and the

importance of relying on faith in God. She had come with me to
Philadelphia a few times and desired to start something like TKJ
in Pottstown, Pennsylvania, where she lived.

I told her that I would be glad to help her
find an appropriate way to serve the poor of
Pottstown in Jesus' name. But I added that
it might not look just like our ministry in
Philadelphia.

EDUCATE
Learn how poverty
affects real people,
and then ask others
to help. Make sure
that you cast your
vote for politicians
who feel that poverty
is a key campaign
issue, and lobby
elected officials to
vote for a budget that
prioritizes aid to the
impoverished.

To find out what was needed in Pottstown,
I spent two solid weeks there. I interviewed
the various social service agencies that were
helping the poor, the churches that served
free dinners, the Salvation Army shelter, and
so on. I went to various parts of town to
observe the different types of people hanging
out there. I went to the housing project in
Stowe (adjacent to Pottstown) to check out
the environment. I talked to the people I
knew in the house churches. I asked the
prison inmates who were from Pottstown
what they thought was needed. I found out
that the only day without any sort of free
food was Wednesday. This presented a challenge because that was
the same night that we served in Philadelphia. I also discovered that
there was a sizable population of homeless teens, who were very
secretive for fear of being incarcerated or returned to abusive homes.
All this research would avoid duplication of the things that were
already being done. However, we wanted to be involved personally
in serving others in Jesus' name.

We found that there were two main sites in Pottstown that

served food—especially emphasizing children's needs—along with a drop-off location to give clothes, food, and toiletries to the teens. Nanci and I prayed and then approached her church to recruit more volunteers. Within a week, we had a full crew, including some sandwich makers, an occasional soup maker, and two drivers. The following week, we did a trial run. We served beanie-weanies, peanut-butter-and-jelly sandwiches, and fruit punch in an empty lot in Pottstown and on the street in the project in Stowe. We served more than one hundred people, mostly children, and left the extra food for the teens to pick up. It went very well. The people were grateful. It was different from Philadelphia—instead of homeless people, there were a lot of children from lower-income families.

ACTIVATE

• Volunteer for a street ministry or homeless shelter.

• Get to know homeless people in your community.

• Help build homes with organizations like Habitat for Humanity, at home and abroad.

Nanci took on the project and served every Wednesday night. Sometimes she would call me on Thursday morning, panicked, saying, "I am out of peanut butter. What am I going to do for next week?"

I would ask her, "What day is it?"

"Thursday."

I would tell her, "We don't need peanut butter for another six days. 'Be anxious for nothing.' God will provide."

The next time Nanci ran out of peanut butter, she waited until Friday to call me, and we had a similar conversation. God always provided.

I also told Nanci that it really wasn't her problem—it was God's. "It is acceptable according to what a man has, not what he has not." If she didn't have peanut butter, it was because God was providing something better for the children that week. Nanci continued to learn, waiting until Tuesday morning to call if she was out of something.

Then one week I got a call on Thursday morning. Nanci said, "I had to call you. Last night as I was on my way to serve the people, and I was worried because I had used the last of the peanut butter. I knew I was wrong to worry, so I asked God to please supply more. Well, when I got home, I couldn't get into my apartment, because the entire front step was covered with jars and jars of peanut butter! O me of little faith!"

Nanci continued to serve every Wednesday night until she passed away from a heart attack on September 4, 1993, at age fifty. May her memory be eternal!

HOW TO ENGAGE IN MEANINGFUL STREET MINISTRY

Nanci's story includes some very important lessons about how to start a ministry. My personal motto is: If I can't do it in Jesus' name, I don't have time to do it. Our ministry will never solicit government funds or accept funds from United Way or any other agency that would restrict our freedom to share our faith in Jesus Christ. I always try to find ways for people to get involved in bite-size ways. For instance, children in Vacation Bible School make power packs for us to give away to the homeless. These are paper bags that the children decorate and fill with a box drink, a granola bar, raisins, perhaps a small tube of toothpaste, etc. Various people make sandwiches. Each week, I don't even know who helps out.

Bathe the ministry in prayer. Honor and respect the people you serve. It is by their prayers that you will be saved.

If you want to have staying power as a servant of the poor, leave idealism behind. The first sin I confessed to God before my priest when I became Orthodox was the sin of idealism. I touched on this before, when I was talking about the dispute over the causes of homelessness. Homelessness is embarrassing to a society that is so affluent. It is easy to develop a theory about the cause, assign blame, and then say, *If we only did this or that, we could solve the problem.* Idealism as a form of idolatry because it substitutes something less than the love of God as a solution for a problem. Idealism expects certain, quantifiable results. It sees social ills as problems that need to be solved, rather than diseases that need to be healed. It is always saying "if only."

There is homelessness in both socialist and capitalist countries. Poverty and homelessness cannot be completely solved. There is no simple "if only" that will fix this problem. I have seen too many people burn out in ministry among the poor because they were motivated by idealism. Invariably, they became disillusioned. Their "if only's" either didn't work or could never be implemented.

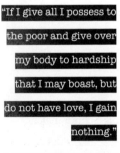

"If I give all I possess to the poor and give over my body to hardship that I may boast, but do not have love, I gain nothing."

—1 CORINTHIANS 13:3, TNIV

Now, I am not hopeless—I do believe that it is possible for homelessness to end. It is a rather recent phenomenon, and we can hope that it will not go on indefinitely. But it is a complex disease caused by sin. The cure is simple to state, but humanly impossible to orchestrate.

Let go of idealism, but trust and obey God. Don't make ending homelessness your goal. Serve the poor in Jesus' name; in so doing, you will help end homelessness. There is always a paradox involved. He that will save his life must lose it.

Both capitalism and socialism treat people as commodities or resources of more or less interchangeable parts, denying the Christian perspective of the unique, intrinsic value of every human being. Add to that the volatility of technological change and globalization, and we have a recipe for disaster. Both capitalism and socialism are idealistic systems that are variations of materialism and antithetical to love. Just look at police dramas on TV. They teach us that there are a lot of bad dudes out there who need to be thrown away, and most of them are young black men. By the nature of our economic systems and technologies reducing the need for manual labor, we don't need so many people to keep the rich in their castles anymore. We also have developed an intolerance for people who are odd. We used to make room for them and find ways to tolerate them.

KENNY

I used to work in a poultry processing plant. A mentally retarded man named Kenny lived across the street from it. The owners of the plant, who lived behind it, hired Kenny and gave him a repetitive job that he could handle. In addition to his wages and benefits, he now had something to do with his time.

Kenny had a habit of sometimes wearing nothing under his white lab coat. Workers in the factory generally knew that he was a few bricks short of a load and would deal with it in a kind and jovial manner. One day, however, he opened his lab coat and flashed a woman working on the line. Instead of explaining to the alarmed but hardly traumatized worker that this fellow had the social maturity of a four-year-old and should be treated as such, they fired the man, fearing a lawsuit.

I recently saw Kenny at a friend's funeral, more than twenty years after his firing. I didn't work in his department. I was just one of hundreds of other employees who passed by him on the way to and from their departments. He greeted me by name immediately, like only a day had passed. He knows the name of everyone he has ever met, no matter how briefly. There is something godly about that.

THE CURE FOR HOMELESSNESS

Divorce has become so common and so easy. It's no big thing to throw a spouse out of the picture—why can't I just walk away from a brother or sister who is difficult or messy, or a mom or dad who is needy, or a son or daughter who has issues? Don't I deserve to be happy? Life would be so much easier without them. The first and most important element of the cure for homelessness is to love God—let Him help you love your family. Be a home-builder. Be the ounce of prevention. Then love your neighbor. We have seen an eighty-three-year-old woman living on the streets for the last few months. She has no children. Why has no neighbor taken her in? That's the way it used to be done. She would be someone's Aunt Margaret and live in Bobby's old room. This is not a radical concept.

When I serve the people on the street, I am not there to preach to them. I don't make them sit or stand through a message and a song before we serve the food. These people are not rats, and the food is not bait. The sharing of food and clothing is not just a means to gather a crowd to evangelize. If I were to do that, it would be a con, not love. I'm sure if I were to preach and give an invitation, many would come forward. The next week I would have the same people responding. I have seen this played out in the prisons. These people will give you what you want if that means you will keep coming. They have now paid for their meal, instead of receiving it as mercy. We do what we do at TKJ not out of idealism to save the world; we do what we do because God honestly loves these wonderful, amazing people and because He won't let us *not* do this. I am not here to save them. They do more to save me.

When they ask me why we help them, why we come out in the rain and snow, why we come back after witnessing violence, why we come back after being hassled and threatened by the police, I tell them that Jesus loves them and that He won't leave me alone if I don't do this. His love compels me. You see, my motives are that of a selfish sinner who is being redeemed and healed by the love of God. This same grace is available to them through Jesus Christ. This is the gospel.

According to Ephesians 2:10, God has prepared good works for us to do. If you want to get involved in service, go out and do something. Anything. Don't expect God to lead you into the ministry that is right for you if you are sitting there, waiting. Have you ever tried to steer a parked car? It is next

PRAY

Lord, You said there would be poor always, yet You admonished us to care for the "least of these." Please help us to love and nurture all those in need—both in faraway lands who hunger and thirst and are ill due to nationwide poverty and those in our hometowns who, because of physical or mental illness or other reasons, need their brothers and sisters to lift them up—never judging or condemning or enabling but rather empowering and loving them without abandon. Grant us Your grace, that we may minister to the least of these as Abraham and Sarah ministered to the angels who came to dine in their home and as the Christians of the early Church ministered to and cared for their brethren. Amen.

to impossible and fairly pointless. So get out and start doing some good works in Jesus' name. You will be amazed at how God leads you to what is right for you.

The cure for homelessness and poverty and war and racism is the total love of God. Musician Todd Rundgren is right: "Love is the Answer."

CRANFORD JOSEPH COULTER serves as the founder and director of The King's Jubilee, a ministry to the poor in Philadelphia, and owns Come and See Icons, Books & Art. He is webmaster for *www.comeandseeicons.com*, *www.shoutforjoy.net*, and *www.orthodoxdelmar.org*. He and his wife, Bethann, live in East Greenville, Pennsylvania, and attend Saint Philip Antiochian Orthodox Church in Souderton with their four daughters, two sons-in-law, and two grandchildren.

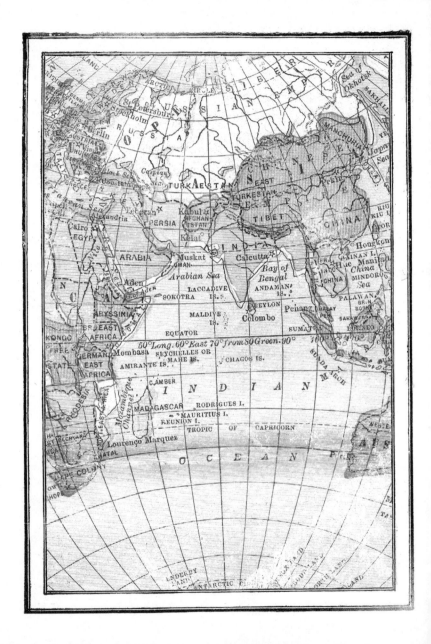

AFTERWORD
WE CAN CHANGE THE WORLD

BY RONALD J. SIDER

"'BUT *NOW*,' SAYS THE ONCE-LER, 'NOW THAT
YOU'RE HERE, THE WORD OF THE LORAX
SEEMS PERFECTLY CLEAR. UNLESS SOMEONE
LIKE YOU CARES A WHOLE AWFUL LOT,
NOTHING IS GOING TO GET BETTER. IT'S NOT.'"
—DR. SEUSS, FROM *THE LORAX*

History demonstrates that blatant evil can be conquered. In my lifetime I have watched Solidarity's bold Polish workers defy a seemingly invincible Soviet system and eventually contribute to the collapse of the Soviet Union. I have watched courageous, nonviolent Filipinos lie down before powerful tanks and overthrow a vicious dictator. I have watched, even played a tiny role, as a global coalition of activists helped daring South Africans bring down a powerful, decades-long system of apartheid.

A longer historical perspective underlines the fact that there is nothing inevitable and unchangeable about widespread injustice. William Wilberforce and his small band of supporters worked tirelessly both inside and outside Parliament for more than thirty years—eventually persuading the British Empire to abolish the slave trade and then slavery itself. At the time when my ancestors, the sixteenth-century Anabaptists, championed religious freedom and were executed by the thousands for their beliefs, they could not foresee that two and a half centuries later, the authors of the American Constitution would place religious freedom at the center of their grand experiment and that over the course of the next two hundred years, religious freedom would become the norm rather than the exception around the world.

A handful of daring nineteenth-century Christian feminists set in place a revolution that continues to spread everywhere, bringing women vastly expanded progress toward equality of opportunity. Gandhi's nonviolent marchers conquered the British Empire. Martin Luther King Jr.'s bold, nonviolent civil rights movement ended legal segregation and brought vastly expanded opportunity for African Americans.

None of these movements brought utopia. Sin and selfishness persist. Injustice continues. But the evidence is clear. Things can change. Unjust structures can be demolished. Faithful, bold, persistent movements can move society toward greater justice.

Christians know that when society changes for the better, God is pleased. The Lord of history works in history to nurture justice and calls on His people to join in the struggle.

The Creator made men and women in His very image, and then assigned us the task of being stewards to watch over and care for the gorgeous garden He had created (Gen. 2:15). God called us to be co-workers, slowly discovering His stunningly complex design in the natural order and then using that growing knowledge to shape civilizations of beauty and goodness. Sin, of course, has messed up everything. But if the history of Israel teaches us anything, it's that history is a dialogue between God and free, responsible persons and that God keeps summoning us again and again to empower the poor and needy and to nurture justice.

There are hundreds of biblical verses that talk about God's concern for the poor. [See chapter 3 of my books *Rich Christians in an Age of Hunger* (5th ed., W Publishing, 2005) and *For They Shall Be Fed* (Word, 1997).] God sent prophets not only to warn Israel and Judah of coming catastrophe because of their idolatry and injustice, but also to promise a future time when the Messiah would come. In that day, there would be peace and justice for the poor.

When Jesus came, He claimed to be that long-expected Messiah. He loved and cared for the whole person. He warned His disciples that if they did not feed the hungry and clothe the naked, they would go to hell (Matt. 25). Most exciting, He promised that the Messianic kingdom, which He said was now breaking into history visibly and powerfully in His growing circle of disciples, would grow larger like a mustard seed. He taught His disciples to pray that God's kingdom would come—that God's will would be done on earth as in heaven. He taught that, in the power of the Holy Spirit, His followers could already begin to live that way in dramatic (albeit imperfect) fashion and then promised that at some time in the future He would return to complete the victory over all sin and injustice. At that time, even the groaning creation will be freed of its bondage to decay (Rom. 8:21). All tears and injustice will disappear, and the kingdoms of this world will become the kingdom of our Lord and Christ.

I have been working for social justice for more than four decades.

We have won some battles, and lost others! People have asked me: "What keeps you going, Ron?" The answer is simple. Jesus rose from the dead and promises to return sometime in the future to complete His victory over evil and injustice. I know where history is going. The final word is not the victory of injustice. The final word is the return of the Resurrected One, who will wipe all tears from our eyes.

But you and I live in the "in-between" time—between the dramatic inbreaking of the kingdom of God in Jesus' life, death and resurrection and its completion at His return.

So what do we do now? We pray hard and work hard.

Let us never suppose that success depends on our diligence and brilliance. This is finally God's task. Of course, we should work hard. We are God's stewards, and God wants to change history through our faithful efforts. But the task is finally the work of Almighty God, the Lord of history, the present and coming King. As such, we should pray as hard for our campaigns for social justice as the wonderful people in a Billy Graham evangelistic campaign have prayed for evangelism. And we should combine our prayer with our most brilliant strategic thinking and most persistent hard work. When God uses our efforts to expand religious freedom, democratic governance, fair legal systems, and socioeconomic justice, let us give thanks to the One who empowers and sustains us. And when we face setbacks, we should remember they are only temporary. Jesus has burst from the tomb. Jesus has already won the decisive victory over all evil. He will most assuredly, as He promised, return someday to complete His victory.

RONALD J. SIDER (PhD, Yale) is a professor of theology, holistic ministry, and public policy; director of the Sider Center on Ministry and Public Policy at Eastern Baptist Theological Seminary; and president of Evangelicals for Social Action. He is the author of twenty-seven books, including *Rich Christians in an Age of Hunger*, which was recognized by *Christianity Today* as one of the one hundred most influential religious books of the twentieth century. Sider is the publisher of *PRISM* magazine and a contributing editor of *Christianity Today* and *Sojourners*.

APPENDIX A

MORE WAYS TO TAKE ACTION

In the chapters within this book, each author outlined concrete ways "to change your world." Here are additional ideas to jump-start your own social-justice journey.

☐ Mentor a young person

☐ Writer a letter to a congressperson about an issue that troubles you

☐ Memorize Scripture relating to social justice

☐ Check out websites like *www.volunteermatch.org* and *www.211.org* that connect willing volunteers with opportunities to serve

☐ Go on a short-term missions trip in lieu of a vacation

☐ If the means exist, plant an organic garden and share the fruits of your harvest with friends, neighbors, and the poor

☐ Choose a social justice-oriented career

☐ Help your neighbors

- [ ] Visit an elderly person in your life

- [ ] Bring a home-cooked meal to parents of a newborn or someone who is suffering from a serious illness

- [ ] Visit shut-ins

- [ ] Get active in local politics

- [ ] Vote in all elections

- [ ] Donate money to small charities

- [ ] Support the notion of community

- [ ] Read to someone in a nursing home

- [ ] Find time to volunteer, even when there is no time

- [ ] Pray throughout the day for the needs of others

- [ ] Become a foster parent

- [ ] Try virtual volunteering— which can include writing press releases, graphic design, online mentoring, and answering counseling hotlines through virtual phone banks

- [ ] Take a panhandler out for a meal—and get to know him or her

- [ ] Go to a conference on social justice

- [ ] Volunteer at a hospice

- [ ] Fold clothes at a nonprofit thrift store

- [ ] When possible, get to know the people you serve—take a relational approach to service

- [ ] Volunteer at a crisis childcare center

☐ When you give, don't expect any kind of reward for your good works

☐ Volunteer in a soup kitchen, food pantry, or homeless shelter

☐ Fast, and then give extra money to an international hunger charity

☐ Buy only what you need—and define your needs conservatively

☐ Give the coat on your back to someone cold on the street

☐ If you see a homeless person stuck in the rain, give him your umbrella

☐ Don't let old clothes hang in your closet—give them away in a clothing drive

☐ Organize a fundraiser for a local charity

☐ Answer a suicide hotline

☐ Read about the lives of the saints: their simple, selfless ways will move you

☐ Study the writings of the Church fathers and mothers—often, their admonishments about serving those in need are just the kick in the pants one needs to do something

☐ Always remember the daily needs of small charities—they suffer most for want of donations when big crises draw donations away

☐ Become a first responder

☐ Research what organizations have the least amount of overhead, and give to them first

- ☐ Bike or walk whenever possible

- ☐ Volunteer to restore a prairie or forest, or get involved with other environmental restoration projects

- ☐ Pick up litter

- ☐ Invest less in indulgences and more in the basic needs of others

- ☐ Teach others how to serve—and primarily, teach by example

- ☐ Show your children the importance of giving

- ☐ Travel—observe, report, and advocate

- ☐ Become involved in your church or denominational anti-hunger program—if your church doesn't have an anti-hunger program, start one

- ☐ Shop conscientiously

- ☐ Sponsor a poor woman or child

- ☐ Educate yourself on social injustices around the world

- ☐ Don't horde your money—be generous with it

- ☐ Tithe

- ☐ Write letters to representatives regarding prohibiting the use of torture and abusive detention in the war on terror

- ☐ Take a trip and see the difference Fair Trade is making in cooperative communities

- ☐ Try everything on this list at least once—then do them over and over again ...

APPENDIX B

DIG DEEPER

SCRIPTURE ON MERCY AND JUSTICE

What follows is a selection of passages from the Bible related to social justice. This is just the tip of the iceberg, though; the Bible is full of hidden gems when it comes to wisdom on charity, philanthropy, and self-sacrificial service of one's neighbors. If you're feeling ambitious, you might try reading three or four chapters in the Bible every night for a year (that's about how long it will take to get through the whole book). As you read, make a note of any passage that deals with social justice. It is amazing how prominent a theme social justice is in the Good Book—especially given how quickly many Christians forget the importance of serving our neighbors as we squabble over theological minutiae, worship styles, politics, and everything else under the sun. Dive into these stirring passages and let them motivate you to take action.

EXODUS 23:6
LEVITICUS 19:15
DEUTERONOMY 14:29

DEUTERONOMY 15:11
PSALM 112:5
PSALM 146:5-8
PROVERBS 10:12
PROVERBS 11:24
PROVERBS 14:31
PROVERBS 22:16
PROVERBS 28:27
ISAIAH 25:1-12
ISAIAH 58:6-10
EZEKIEL 18:5-7
MATTHEW 6:1-4
MATTHEW 19:21
MATTHEW 25:31-45
MARK 12:31
MARK 12:41-44
LUKE 10:25-37
LUKE 11:39-42
LUKE 12:32-34
LUKE 14:12-14
JOHN 15:13
ACTS 4:32-35
ROMANS 13:9
1 CORINTHIANS 13:3
2 CORINTHIANS 9:7
JAMES 1:27
JAMES 2:14-18

APPENDIX C

RESOURCES

According to the National Center for Charitable Statistics, in 2004 there were 119,515 tax-exempt 501(c)(3), nonprofits dealing with social welfare registered with the U.S. government. That doesn't include many church ministries and unregistered local efforts to serve those in need. In other words, if you're looking for ways to serve, opportunities abound. A quick Google search will yield hundreds upon hundreds of ways to get involved, from your local street ministry or parish clothing drive to the big national and international nonprofits. Here is a listing of some of the larger organizations dealing with all different kinds of social justice issues. Check them out, and then do your own search. Find something that suits your talents and get plugged in!

ACTING ON AIDS

www.actingonaids.org

marketing-pr@actingonaids.org

Acting on AIDS is a national awareness and activism campaign spreading across Christian colleges through which students mobilize other students to do something about the global AIDS pandemic.

ACTION AGAINST HUNGER

www.aah-usa.org

info@actionagainsthunger.org

Action Against Hunger delivers programs in more than forty countries, specializing in emergency situations of war, conflict, and natural disasters and longer-term assistance to people in distress.

AFRICAN FAITH AND JUSTICE NETWORK

www.afjn.cua.edu

afjn@afjn.org

The Africa Faith and Justice Network strives to be a meaningful voice for Africa in U.S. public policy. AFJN works closely with Catholic missionary congregations and numerous Africa-focused coalitions of all persuasions to advocate for U.S. economic and political policies that will benefit Africa's poor majority, facilitate an end to armed conflict, establish equitable trade and investment with Africa, and promote ecologically sound development.

AFRICAN LEADERSHIP

www.africanleadership.org

African Leadership is committed to developing projects and programs that meet both the physical and spiritual needs of Africans.

AFRICAN WELL FUND

www.africanwellfund.org

info@africanwellfund.org

African Well Fund is dedicated to raising funds for building and maintaining wells in Africa. It was formed in October 2002 by a group of U2 fans inspired by the media coverage of Bono's May 2002 trip to Africa with then Secretary of U.S. Treasury, Paul O'Neill.

AFRICARE

www.africare.org

development@africare.org

Africare's programs address needs in the principal areas of food security and agriculture as well as health and HIV/AIDS. Africare also supports water resource development, environmental management, basic education, microenterprise development, governance initiatives, and emergency humanitarian aid.

AMERICAN LEPROSY MISSIONS

www.leprosy.org

amlep@leprosy.org

American Leprosy Missions (ALM) is a nondenominational Christian ministry that provides care to people around the world with leprosy and Buruli ulcer and related disabilities.

AMERICA'S SECOND HARVEST
www.secondharvest.org

America's Second Harvest distributes food and grocery products through a nationwide network of certified affiliates, increases public awareness of domestic hunger, and advocates for policies that benefit America's hungry.

BAPTIST PEACE FELLOWSHIP OF NORTH AMERICA
www.bpfna.org
bpfna@bpfna.org

The Baptist Peace Fellowship of North America gathers, equips, and mobilizes Baptists to build a culture of peace rooted in justice.

BE A WITNESS
www. beawitness.org/home
info@beawitness.org

The BeAWitness.org campaign focuses on ensuring that TV networks pay attention to the genocide unfolding in the Darfur region of Sudan.

BLOOD:WATER MISSION
www.bloodwatermission.com
bloodwater@bloodwatermission.com

Blood:Water Mission is committed to fighting the HIV/AIDS pandemic by building clean wells in Africa, supporting medical facilities caring for the sick, and making a lasting impact in the fight against poverty, injustice, and oppression in Africa through the linking of needs, talents, and continents with people and resources.

BREAD FOR THE WORLD
www.bread.org
bread@bread.org

Bread for the World is a nationwide Christian citizens movement seeking justice for the world's hungry people by lobbying our nation's decision makers. BFW Institute seeks justice for hungry people by engaging in research and education on policies related to hunger and development.

CALL TO RENEWAL
www.calltorenewal.org
ctr@calltorenewal.org

Call to Renewal is a national network of churches, faith-based organizations, and individuals working to overcome poverty in America. Through local and national partnerships with groups from across the theological and political spectrum, CTR convenes the broadest table of Christians focused on anti-poverty efforts.

CARE

www.careusa.org

info@care.org

CARE works with poor communities in more than seventy countries around the world to find lasting solutions to poverty.

CATHOLIC CHARITIES

www.catholiccharitiesusa.org

Catholic Charities USA is the membership association of one of the nation's largest social service networks. It supports and enhances the work of its membership by providing networking opportunities, national advocacy and media efforts, program development, training and technical assistance, and financial support.

CATHOLIC RELIEF SERVICES

www.catholicrelief.org

webmaster@catholicrelief.org

Catholic Relief Services assists the poor and disadvantaged, leveraging the teachings of the Gospel of Jesus Christ to alleviate human suffering, promote development of all people, and foster charity and justice throughout the world.

THE CENTER ON PHILANTHROPY AT INDIANA UNIVERSITY

www.philanthropy.iupui.edu

psinfo@iupui.edu

The Center on Philanthropy at Indiana University increases the understanding of philanthropy and improves its practice through programs in research, teaching, public service, and public affairs. The center has academic and research programs on the IUPUI and the IU–Bloomington campuses.

THE CENTER FOR PUBLIC JUSTICE

www.cpjustice.org

inquiries@cpjustice.org

The Center for Public Justice is an independent organization for policy research and civic education. Its mission is to equip citizens, develop leaders, and shape policy.

CHILDFUND INTERNATIONAL

www.childfundinternational.org

info@childfundinternational.org

ChildFund International is an alliance of global, developmental child-sponsorship organizations that implement lasting and meaningful changes in the lives of impoverished children and families worldwide.

CHILDREN'S DEFENSE FUND

www.childrensdefense.org

cdfinfo@childrensdefense.org

Children's Defense Fund provides

a strong, effective voice for all the children of America who cannot vote, lobby, or speak for themselves. CDF pays particular attention to the needs of poor and minority children and those with disabilities. CDF educates the nation about the needs of children and encourages preventive investment before they become sick, get into trouble, drop out of school, or suffer family breakdown.

CHRISTIAN CHILDREN'S FUND

www.christianchildrensfund.org

questions@ccfusa.org

Christian Children's Fund creates an environment of hope and respect for children in need, giving them opportunities to achieve their full potential and providing children, families, and communities with practical tools for positive change.

CHRISTIAN PEACEMAKER TEAMS

www.cpt.org

peacemakers@cpt.org

Christian Peacemaker Teams offers an organized, nonviolent alternative to war and other forms of lethal inter-group conflict.

CHRISTIAN REFORMED WORLD RELIEF COMMITTEE

www.crwrc.org

crwrc@crcna.org

The Christian Reformed World Relief Committee is a relief, development, and educational ministry of the Christian Reformed Church in North America. CRWRC partners with local agencies that understand local needs. Together, CRWRC and its partners find ways to provide lasting change for people in more than thirty countries around the world.

CHURCH WORLD SERVICE

www.churchworldservice.org

info@churchworldservice.org

Church World Service is the relief, development, and refugee assistance ministry of thirty-six Protestant, Orthodox, and Anglican denominations in the United States. Working in partnership with indigenous organizations in more than eighty countries, CWS works worldwide to meet human needs and foster self-reliance for those in difficult circumstances.

COALITION OF HUMAN NEEDS

www.chn.org

ahughes@chn.org

The Coalition on Human Needs is an alliance of national organizations working together to promote public policies that address the needs of low-income and other vulnerable populations.

COMPASSION INTERNATIONAL
www.compassion.com

Compassion International exists as an advocate for children, releasing them from spiritual, economic, social, and physical poverty and enabling them to become responsible, fulfilled Christian adults.

CONVOY OF HOPE
www.convoyofhope.org
info@convoyofhope.org

Convoy of Hope serves in the United States and around the world providing disaster relief, building supply lines, and sponsoring outreaches to the poor and hurting in communities.

COVERING KIDS & FAMILIES
www.coveringkidsandfamilies.org
info@coveringkidsandfamilies.org
The Robert Wood Johnson Foundation launched Covering Kids & Families (CKF), a four-year, $55 million initiative to increase the number of uninsured children and families who benefit from existing health care coverage programs.

CROSS-CULTURAL SOLUTIONS
www.crossculturalsolutions.org
info@crossculturalsolutions.org

Cross-Cultural Solutions is a registered charity located in Brighton, U.K., that operates in ten countries, offering three types of programs:

Volunteer Abroad, Intern Abroad, and Insight Abroad.

DATA
www.data.org
data@data.org

DATA aims to raise awareness about, and spark response to, the crises swamping Africa: unpayable Debts, uncontrolled spread of AIDS, and unfair Trade rules that keep Africans poor. The organization was founded in 2002 by U2 frontman Bono, along with Bobby Shriver and activists from the Jubilee 2000 Drop the Debt campaign.

DEATH PENALTY INFORMATION CENTER
www.deathpenaltyinfo.org
rdennis@deathpenaltyinfo.org

The Death Penalty Information Center is a nonprofit organization serving the media and the public with analysis and information on issues concerning capital punishment. The center prepares in-depth reports, issues press releases, conducts briefings for journalists, and serves as a resource to those working on this issue.

DIRECT RELIEF INTERNATIONAL
www.directrelief.org
info@directrelief.org

Direct Relief International works to

improve the quality of life for people in need, especially in the area of health, by providing essential material resources to locally run health programs in poor areas around the world and during times of disaster.

EVANGELICAL ENVIRONMENTAL NETWORK

www.creationcare.org

een@creationcare.org

Evangelical Environmental Network is an evangelical ministry whose purpose is to "declare the Lordship of Christ over all creation" (Col. 1:15-20). EEN's flagship publication, *Creation Care* magazine, provides biblically informed and timely articles on topics ranging from how to protect your loved ones against environmental threats to how to more fully praise the Creator for the wonder of His creation.

EVANGELICALS FOR SOCIAL ACTION

www.esa-online.org

ronsider@esa-online.org

Evangelicals for Social Action exists to challenge and equip people in the Church to be agents of God's redemption and transformation in the world. ESA pursues this mission through reflecting on church and society from a biblical perspective, training in holistic ministry, and linking people together for mutual learning and action.

FAIR TRADE RESOURCE NETWORK

www.fairtraderesource.org

info@fairtraderesource.org

The Fair Trade Resource Network's goal is to raise consumer awareness about improving people's lives through Fair Trade alternatives by gathering and compiling research and data about Fair Trade; providing information about Fair Trade to the public, the media, and Fair Trade advocates; and galvanizing Fair Trade organizations and individuals seeking to get involved.

FELLOWSHIP OF RECONCILIATION

www.forusa.org

for@forusa.org

The Fellowship of Reconciliation carries out programs and educational projects concerned with domestic and international peace and justice, nonviolent alternatives to conflict, and the rights of conscience.

FEMINISTS FOR LIFE

www.feministsforlife.org

info@feministsforlife.org

Feminists for Life of America is dedicated to systematically eliminating the root causes that drive women to abortion through holistic, woman-centered solutions.

FIRST 8
www.first8.org
welcome@first8.org

First8.org is a Dutch anti-poverty campaign, based on the eight UN Millennium Development Goals, that uses an interactive website with vivid photography to give a face to poverty.

FLORESTA
www.floresta.org

Floresta is a Christian nonprofit organization that reverses deforestation and poverty in the world by transforming the lives of the rural poor.

FOOD RESOURCE BANK
www.foodsresourcebank.org
laurie@foodsresourcebank.org

Foods Resource Bank works on behalf of its members to mobilize and increase the resources needed for food security projects. Resources are both material ("in-kind") and cash, and are provided to the Christian organizations that are implementing members of FRB. These members work with their in-country partners worldwide to implement assistance.

FREEDOM FROM FEAR
www.freedomfromfear.org.uk
josh@freedomfromfear.org.uk

Freedom from Fear calls for the extension of basic civil freedoms to all people.

FREEDOM FROM HUNGER
www.freedomfromhunger.org
info@freefromhunger.org

Freedom from Hunger is an international development organization working in sixteen countries across the globe, bringing innovative and sustainable self-help solutions to the fight against chronic hunger and poverty.

GENOCIDE INTERVENTION NETWORK
www.genocideinterventionfund.org
info@genocideintervention.net

Genocide Intervention Network aims to increase public awareness of genocide and support organizations, initiatives, and government policies designed to help prevent and stop genocide.

THE GLOBAL FUND TO FIGHT AIDS, TUBERCULOSIS AND MALARIA
www.theglobalfund.org
info@theglobalfund.org

The Global Fund was created to finance a dramatic turnaround in the fight against AIDS, tuberculosis, and malaria.

GLOBAL IMPACT
www.charity.org
mail@charity.org

Global Impact is dedicated to helping the poorest people on earth. It represents more than fifty of the most respected U.S.-based international charities in workplace-giving campaigns across the nation.

GLOBAL VOLUNTEER NETWORK

www.volunteer.org.nz

info@volunteer.org.nz

The Global Volunteer Network offers volunteer opportunities in community projects throughout the world, supporting the work of local community organizations in developing countries through the placement of international volunteers.

HABITAT FOR HUMANITY INTERNATIONAL

www.habitat.org

publicinfo@habitat.org

Habitat for Humanity builds houses for those in need. These houses are sold with no profit made; homeowners contribute "sweat equity," and house payments are recycled to build additional houses.

HOMEBOY INDUSTRIES

www.homeboy-industries.org

info@homeboy-industries.org

Homeboy Industries' mission is to assist at-risk and former gang-involved youth to become contributing members of our community through a variety of services in response to their multiple needs. Free programs—including counseling, education, tattoo removal, job training, and job placement—enable young people to redirect their lives and provide them with hope for their futures.

HUNGER BANQUET

www.hungerbanquet.org

info@oxfamamerica.org

Oxfam's virtual Hunger Banquet gives visitors a chance to learn about hunger from the point of view of those who experience it every day.

INTERNATIONAL CHRISTIAN CONCERN

www.persecution.org

icc@persecution.org

International Christian Concern is a nonprofit, human rights organization dedicated to assisting and sustaining Christians who are victims of persecution and discrimination due to their faith.

INTERNATIONAL JUSTICE MISSION

www.ijm.org

contact@ijm.org

International Justice Mission is a human rights agency that rescues victims of violence, sexual exploitation, slavery, and oppression.

INTERNATIONAL NETWORK OF PRISON MINISTRIES

www.prisonministry.net

The purpose of the International Network of Prison Ministries web site is to bring under one Internet roof all prison ministries worldwide involved in crime prevention and rehabilitation through the Word of God.

INTERNATIONAL ORTHODOX CHRISTIAN CHARITIES

www.iocc.org

relief@iocc.org

International Orthodox Christian Charities is the official humanitarian aid agency of Orthodox Christians to work in cooperation with Orthodox Churches worldwide. The mission of IOCC is to respond to the call of our Lord Jesus Christ, to minister to those who are suffering and in need throughout the world, sharing with them God's gifts of food, shelter, economic self-sufficiency, and hope.

JUBILEE USA

www.jubileeusa.org

coord@jubileeusa.org

Jubilee USA Network began as Jubilee 2000/USA in 1997 when a diverse gathering of people and organizations came together in response to the international call for Jubilee debt cancellation. Now more than sixty organizations—including

labor, churches, religious communities and institutions, AIDS activists, trade campaigners—and more than nine thousand individuals are active members of the Jubilee USA Network. This strong, diverse, and growing network is dedicated to working toward a world free of debt.

LIFEWATER INTERNATIONAL

www.lifewaterinternational.org

info@lifewater.org

Lifewater International demonstrates Jesus' love by working with people in developing countries to improve their quality of life through accessing, using, and maintaining safe water.

LIVING WATERS FOR THE WORLD

www.livingwatersfortheworld.org

info@livingwatersfortheworld.org

The vision of Living Waters for the World is to use the gift of clean water to bring together congregations of the Synod of Living Waters PC (USA)—and others interested in its mission—with their sisters and brothers in need for a life-changing experience with the risen Christ.

LUTHERAN WORLD FEDERATION'S DEPARTMENT FOR WORLD SERVICE

www.lutheranworld.org

mbe@lutheranworld.org

The Department for World Service is the internationally recognized humanitarian and development agency of the Lutheran World Federation. It works with marginalized and disadvantaged communities in the areas of greatest vulnerability and endemic need.

MAKE TRADE FAIR
www.maketradefair.org
maketradefair@oxfamamerica.org

Make Trade Fair is a part of Oxfam International, a confederation of twelve non-governmental organizations working together in more than eighty countries to find lasting solutions to poverty, suffering, and injustice.

MAP INTERNATIONAL
www.map.org

MAP International promotes the total health—physical, economic, social, emotional, and spiritual—of impoverished people in more than 115 countries through the provision of essential medicines, promotion of community health, and prevention and eradication of disease.

MEDAIR
www.medair.org
info@medair.org

Medair is a non-governmental organization that responds to suffering victims in war and disaster situations (especially those whom have been forgotten or neglected) through various kinds of emergency and rehabilitative projects.

MILLENNIUM CAMPAIGN
www.millenniumcampaign.org

An initiative of the United Nations, the Millennium Campaign informs, inspires, and encourages people's involvement and action for the realization of the Millennium Development Goals.

THE MORATORIUM CAMPAIGN
www.moratoriumcampaign.org
info@moratoriumcampaign.org

The Moratorium Campaign works to see every state declare a moratorium on executions. It is currently mapping out a plan of action to help people throughout the country take solid, practical steps toward achieving a moratorium in their state.

MURDER VICTIMS' FAMILIES FOR RECONCILIATION
www.mvfr.org
info@mvfr.org

Murder Victims' Families for Reconciliation is a non-religious death-penalty abolition organization that includes people of a wide variety of faiths and belief systems.

NATIONAL COALITION TO ABOLISH THE DEATH PENALTY

www.ncadp.org

info@ncadp.org

National Coalition to Abolish the Death Penalty is the only fully staffed national organization exclusively devoted to abolishing capital punishment. NCADP provides information, advocates for public policy, and mobilizes and supports individuals and institutions that share their unconditional rejection of capital punishment.

NATIONAL STUDENT CAMPAIGN AGAINST HUNGER AND HOMELESSNESS

www.studentsagainsthunger.org

info@studentsagainsthunger.org

The National Student Campaign Against Hunger and Homelessness is committed to ending hunger and homelessness in America by educating, engaging, and training students to directly meet individuals' immediate needs while advocating for long-term systemic solutions.

NETWORK FOR GOOD

www.networkforgood.org

Network for Good is a leading charitable resource—an e-philanthropy site where individuals can donate, volunteer, and get involved with the issues they care about. The organization's goal is to connect people to charities via the Internet, using the virtual world to deliver real resources to nonprofits and communities.

NONVIOLENT PEACEFORCE

www.nonviolentpeaceforce.org

info@nonviolentpeaceforce.org

The mission of the Nonviolent Peaceforce is to build a trained, international civilian peaceforce committed to nonviolent third-party intervention.

THE ONE CAMPAIGN

www.one.org

one@data.org

ONE is an effort by Americans to rally Americans—ONE by ONE—to fight the emergency of global AIDS and extreme poverty. The ONE Campaign is engaging Americans through a diverse coalition of faith-based and anti-poverty organizers to show the steps people can take, ONE by ONE, to fight global AIDS and poverty.

ORTHODOX PEACE FELLOWSHIP

www.incommunion.org

incommunion@cs.com

Orthodox Peace Fellowship is an association of Orthodox Christians belonging to different nations and jurisdictions trying to live the peace of Christ in day-to-day life, including situations of division and conflict.

OXFAM INTERNATIONAL
www.oxfaminternational.org
info@oxfamamerica.org

Oxfam International is a confederation of twelve organizations working together with more than three thousand partners in more than one hundred countries to find lasting solutions to poverty, suffering, and injustice. Oxfam International seeks increased worldwide public understanding that economic and social justice are crucial to sustainable development.

PAX CHRISTI
www.paxchristi.net
info@paxchristi.net

Pax Christi International is a nonprofit, non-governmental Catholic peace movement working on a global scale on a wide variety of issues in the fields of human rights, security and disarmament, economic justice, and ecology.

PREVENT GENOCIDE INTERNATIONAL
www.preventgenocide.org
info@preventgenocide.org

Prevent Genocide International is a nonprofit educational organization established in 1998 with the purpose of bringing about the elimination of the crime of genocide. The organization makes particular use of the Internet as a way of linking persons around the world in a transnational network of global civic engagement and action. The foremost goal of Prevent Genocide International is to cultivate well-informed and articulate voices in many nations that are able to speak out in the emerging global civil society against the crime of genocide.

PRISON FELLOWSHIP
www.pfm.org

Founded in 1976 by Chuck Colson, Prison Fellowship partners with local churches across the country to minister to a group that society often scorns and neglects: prisoners, ex-prisoners, and their families. The focus of this ministry includes fellowshipping with Jesus (including teaching others to live and look at life from a biblical perspective), visiting prisoners, and welcoming the children of prisoners.

REFORMED CHURCH WORLD SERVICE
www.rcws.rca.org
rcws@rca.org

Reformed Church World Service

is a ministry of compassion and hope. Its purpose is to work with partners to alleviate hunger and poverty and to seek justice for people around the world.

RESTORING EDEN

www.restoringeden.org

info@restoringeden.org

Restoring Eden is dedicated to helping the Christian community love, serve, and protect God's creation.

SAMARITAN'S PURSE

www.samaritanspurse.org

info@samaritan.org

Samaritan's Purse is a nondenominational evangelical Christian organization providing spiritual and physical aid to hurting people around the world.

SAVEASLAVE.COM

www.saveaslave.com

The mission of SaveASlave.com is to inform the world about the issues surrounding modern involuntary servitude and encourage former slaves by providing links to resources for training, financial, and spiritual support.

SERRV INTERNATIONAL

www.serrv.org

marketing@agreatergift.org

SERRV International is a nonprofit alternative trade and development organization that promotes the social and economic progress of people in developing regions of the world by marketing their products in a just and direct manner.

SERVE YOUR WORLD

www.serveyourworld.com

questions@serveyourworld.com

Founded in 2002, ServeYourWorld has quickly become an authority site on volunteering abroad with relevant news, articles, stories, and more. Thousands of former, current, and prospective volunteers visit ServeYourWorld each week. Part web magazine, part travel guide, and part community, ServeYourWorld has information on all aspects of volunteering abroad, from organization reviews to guides on packing.

THE SIMPLE LIVING NETWORK

www.simpleliving.net

service@simpleliving.net

The Simple Living Network website contains tools, examples, and contacts for conscious, simple, healthy, and restorative living.

SOJOURNERS

www.sojo.net

sojourners@sojo.net

Sojourners is a Christian ministry whose mission is to proclaim and practice the biblical call to integrate spiritual renewal and social justice. In response to this call, Sojourners offer a vision for faith in public life by publishing *Sojourners* magazine, *SojoMail*, and other resources that address issues of faith, politics, and culture from a biblical perspective; preaching, teaching, organizing, and public witness; nurturing community by bringing together people from the various traditions and streams of the Church; and hosting an annual program of voluntary service for education, ministry, and discipleship.

TAKING IT GLOBAL
www.takingitglobal.org
info@takingitglobal.org

TakingITGlobal is an online community for young people interested in connecting across cultures and making a difference, with hundreds of thousands of visitors each month. TakingITGlobal works with global partners—from UN agencies to major companies, especially youth organizations—to build the capacity of youth for development, artistic, and media expression, to make education more engaging, and to involve young people in global decision making.

TARGET EARTH
www.targetearth.org
info@targetearth.org

Target Earth is a national movement

of individuals, churches, college fellowships, and Christian ministries motivated by the biblical call to be faithful stewards of everything God created, to love our neighbors as ourselves, and to care for the earth.

TEN THOUSAND VILLAGES
www.tenthousandvillages.org
inquiry.us@tenthousandvillages.com

Ten Thousand Villages provides vital, fair income to third-world people by marketing their handicrafts and telling their stories in North America.

UNICEF
www.unicef.org
information@unicefusa.org

UNICEF was created to overcome the obstacles that poverty, violence, disease, and discrimination place in a child's path.

UNITED STUDENTS AGAINST SWEATSHOPS
www.studentsagainstsweatshops.org
organize@usasnet.org

United Students Against Sweatshops is an international student movement of campuses and individual students fighting for sweatshop-free labor conditions and workers' rights.

UNITED STUDENTS FOR FAIR TRADE

www.usft.org
usft@usft.org

USFT is a national network of student organizations advocating around Fair Trade products, policies, and principles.

WAR CHILD

www.warchild.org
info@warchild.ca

War Child is a network of independent organizations working across the world to help children affected by war. War Child was founded upon a fundamental goal: to advance the cause of peace through investing hope in the lives of children caught up in the horrors of war.

WATERAID

www.wateraid.org.uk
wateraid@wateraid.org

WaterAid is dedicated exclusively to the provision of safe domestic water, sanitation, and hygiene education to the world's poorest people.

WATERCAN

www.watercan.com
info@watercan.com

WaterCan is a registered charity that is dedicated to providing clean drinking water to the world's poorest people.

WaterCan currently supports projects in Africa.

WHAT WOULD JESUS DRIVE

www.whatwouldjesusdrive.org
een@creationcare.org

WWJDrive, organized and sponsored by the Evangelical Environmental Network, exists to help Christians and others understand that our transportation choices are moral choices that fall under the Lordship of Christ, and take appropriate actions to address the problems associated with our transportation choices.

WHEAT RIDGE MINISTRIES

www.wheatridge.org
wrmmaherg@wheatridge.org

Wheat Ridge Ministries is an independent Lutheran charitable organization that provides support for new church-related health and hope ministries.

WITNESS FOR PEACE

www.witnessforpeace.org
witness@witnessforpeace.org

Witness for Peace supports peace, justice, and sustainable economies in the Americas by changing U.S. policies and corporate practices that contribute to poverty and oppression in Latin America and the Caribbean.

WOMEN FOR WOMEN INTERNATIONAL

www.womenforwomen.org

general@womenforwomen.org

Women for Women International was founded in 1993 to help women overcome the horrors of war and civil strife in ways that can help them rebuild their lives, families, and communities. Women for Women International has direct experience in Croatia, Bosnia and Herzegovina, Rwanda, Kosovo, Bangladesh, Nigeria, Colombia, Pakistan, Afghanistan, Iraq, and the Democratic Republic of the Congo.

WORLD RELIEF

www.wr.org

worldrelief@wr.org

The mission of World Relief is to work with, for, and from the Church to relieve human suffering, poverty, and hunger worldwide in the name of Jesus Christ.

WORLD VISION

www.worldvision.org

info@worldvision.org

World Vision's mission is to call people to a life-changing commitment to serve the poor in the name of Christ.

YOUTH WITH A MISSION

www.ywam.org

nao@ywam.org

Youth With A Mission is an international movement of Christians from many denominations dedicated to serving Jesus throughout the world. YWAM's ministries fit into three main categories: evangelism, training, and mercy ministry.

NOTES

INTRODUCTION

1. Jose Luis Gonzales-Balado and Janet N. Playfoot, eds., *My Life for the Poor* (San Francisco: Harper and Row Publishers, 1985), 32.

CHAPTER 3: WOMEN'S RIGHTS

1. House Committee on International Relations, Population Control in China: Hearing before the International Operations and Human Rights Subcommittee of the International Relations Committee, 104th Cong., 1st sess., 1995, 63.

2. Personal story as told to author. Unless otherwise noted, vignettes in this article are based on personal encounters by the author or other members of Feminists for Life.

3. Millennium Campaign, "Goal 1: Eradicate Hunger and Extreme Poverty," United Nations, *http://www.millenniumcampaign.org/site/pp.asp?c=grKVL2NLE&b= 185518* (accessed August 30, 2005).

4. *The Revolution*, 4(1):4, July 8, 1869.

5. Alan Guttmacher Institute, Facts in Brief: Induced Abortion, 2003.

6. "Further Evidence of Prolife Sentiment up to the Present Wave of Feminism," *Prolife Feminism Yesterday and Today*, eds. Mary Krane Derr, Rachel MacNair, Linda Naranjo-Huebl (New York: Sulzburger & Graham Publishing, 1995), 136.

7. Millennium Campaign, "Goal 3: Promote Gender Equality and Empower Women," United Nations, *http://www.millenniumcampaign.org/site/pp.asp?c= grKVL2NLE&b=186382* (accessed August 30, 2005).

8. U.S. Department of State, "Country Reports on Human Rights Practices 2004 El Salvador," February 28, 2005.

9. U.S. Department of State, Office to Monitor and Combat Trafficking in Persons, Trafficking in Persons Report, June 2005, 5.

10. United Nations, Investigation by the Office of Internal Oversight Services into allegations of sexual exploitation and abuse in the United Nations Organization Mission in the Democratic Republic of the Congo, 59th sess., January 5, 2005, 10.

11. Donna St. George, "CDC Explores Pregnancy-Homicide Link," *Washington Post*, February 23, 2005, *http://www.washingtonpost.com/ac2/wp-dyn/A45626-2005Feb22*

12. "Child soldiers: A global issue," Amnesty International, *http://web.amnesty.org/pages/childsoldiers-background-eng* (accessed August 30, 2005).

13. Trafficking in Persons Report, June 2005: 5.

14. U.S. Department of State, "Country Reports on Human Rights Practices 2003, China," Section 5: Discrimination Based on Race, Sex, Disability, Language, or Social Status (February 25, 2004), *http://www.state.gov/g/drl/rls/hrrpt/2003/27768.htm* (accessed August 30, 2005).

15. Rebecca Allison and Justin McCurry, "40m bachelors and no women ... the birth of a new problem for China," *The Guardian*, March 9, 2004.

16. Bernard Nathanson, *Aborting America* (New York: Doubleday, 1979), 193.

17. Center for Disease Control, National Center for Health Statistics, Supplement to the Monthly Vital Statistics Report: Advance Reports 1986: Series 24, Complications of Data on Natality, Mortality, Marriage, Divorce, and Induced Terminations of Pregnancy, No. 3, Vital and Health Statistics.

18. Kristen Aiken, "Dutch doctors admit infant euthanasia," May 25, 2005, *http://www.abc.net.au/pm/content/2005/s1377030.htm*.

CHAPTER 4: FAIR TRADE

1. Charis Gresser and Sophia Tickell, "Pobreza em Sua Xícara: O Que Há Por Trás da Crise do Café," Oxfam International, Geneva: 2002.

2. Chris Bacon, "Confronting the Coffee Crisis: Can Fair Trade, Organic, and Specialty Coffees Reduce Small-Scale Farmer Vulnerability in Northern Nicaragua?" *World Development*.

3. Gresser and Tickell.

4. Bacon.

5. Gresser and Tickell.

6. Laura Raynolds, "Re-Embedding Global Agriculture: The International Organic and Fair Trade Movements," Agriculture and Human Values, 17:297-309, 2000.

7. Evi Mateboer, International Fairtrade Labelling Organization, pers. comm., November 21, 2003.

CHAPTER 5: HUNGER

1. "Halving hunger: it can be done (summary final report)," UN Millennium Project Hunger Task Force 2005.

2. Mark Nord, Margaret Andrews, and Susan Carlson, "Household Food Security in the United States, 2003," ERS Research Brief, Economic Research Service, October 2004.

3. Marc Cohen, *What Governments Can Do: Hunger 1997*, Bread for the World Institute.

4. Hunger and Homelessness Survey 2004, U.S. Conference of Mayors—Sodexho USA, December 2004.

5. Marc Cohen

6. America's Second Harvest, *http://www.secondharvest.org*.

7. Marc Cohen, *Hunger in a Global Economy: Hunger 1998*, Bread for the World Institute.

8. Barry Bearak, "Why People Still Starve," *The New York Times*, July 13, 2003.

9. Marc. J. Cohen and Jashinta D'Costa, "Overview of World Hunger," *What Governments Can Do: Hunger 1997* (Silver Spring, Md.: Bread for the World Institute, 1996), 23.

10. "Halving hunger: it can be done."

CHAPTER 6: HIV/AIDS

1. "2004 Report on the global AIDS epidemic," Joint United Nations Programme on HIV/AIDS (UNAIDS), *http://www.unaids.org/bangkok2004/GAR2004_html/GAR2004_00_en.htm*.

2. Ibid.

CHAPTER 8: WAR AND PEACE

1. Roland H. Bainton, *Christian Attitudes Toward War and Peace* (Abingdon Press, 1960).

2. Richard McSorley, *The New Testament Basis of Peacemaking* (Herald Press, 1985).

3. Christian Classics Ethereal Library at Calvin College, *http://www.ccel.org/ccel/schaff/npnf110.html*.

4. Rob Yule, "The Politics of Jesus," St. Albans Presbyterian Church, Palmerston North, New Zealand, March 2, 1997.

5. Mohandas K. Gandhi, *The Story of My Experiments with Truth* (Beacon Press, 1993).

6. David Christie, "An Effective Response to Terrorism," *Today*, July 2004.

7. Peter Ackerman and Jack DuVall, *A Force More Powerful* (St. Martin's Press/Palgrave, 2000) and the film by the same name produced by Steve York (2000). For more information, go to *http://www.aforcemorepowerful.org*.

8. Glen Stassen, Ed., *Just Peacemaking: Ten Practices for Abolishing War* (Pilgrim Press, 1998).

CHAPTER 10: THE ENVIRONMENT

1. "Burden of Disease Increased by Environmental Degradation," World Bank, October 5, 2005, *http://web.worldbank.org/WBSITE/EXTERNAL/TOPICS/ ENVIRONMENT/0,,contentMDK:20672727~menuPK:64021753~ pagePK:64020865~piPK:149114~theSitePK:244381,00.html0,,contentMDK: 20672727~menuPK:64021753~pagePK:64020865~piPK:149114~theSitePK: 244381,00.html.*
2. Press conference, *http://www.whitehouse.gov/news/briefings/20010507.html.*
3. "In This Place: A Guide for Those Who Would Work in the Country of the Kaktovikmiut (An Unfinished and Ongoing Work of the People of Kaktovik, Alaska)."
4. Ruth Goring, "Evangelicals for Social Action," *Prism* Magazine, 11, no. 3 (May/June 2004).
5. Ibid.

ACKNOWLEDGMENTS

Given my lack of experience with social justice, I could absolutely not have put together this book without the help of several wiser, more experienced folks. They include friend and University of Illinois government-documents librarian David Griffiths; the wonderful writers and their assistants, who very graciously took time out of extremely busy schedules to contribute essays; the editors of *RELEVANT* magazine, who believe so passionately in social justice; and all the folks I've interviewed or called upon at any point as I researched this book—you know who you are, and I thank you. I also thank my wonderful husband and our precious daughters for their patience with me during the long hours I spent glued to my laptop. I thank my spiritual father, Rev. George Pyle, for giving me his blessing to put together this book; and finally, I humbly thank our good Lord, who heard and answered my prayers all along the way.

This broad group of writers comment specifically on areas where they have personal and professional experience. Participation in this book does not imply that all of the writers would agree wholeheartedly with the views of other contributors, nor do the organizations the writers represent necessarily endorse the views of all the contributors.